W0082433

Habits of the Rich

Juan Diego Gómez Gómez

Habits of the Rich

New ideas for achieving
financial freedom

PAIDÓS EMPRESA

Work edited in collaboration with Editorial Planeta – Colombia

Cover and collection design: Department of Editorial Design, Editorial Planeta Colombiana

Original title: *Hábitos de ricos. Nuevas ideas para alcanzar la libertad financiera*

Translated from the Spanish by Cecile Dunn

© 2019, Juan Diego Gómez Gómez

© Editorial Planeta Colombiana, S.A.

All Rights Reserved

© 2019, Ediciones Culturales Paidós, S.A. de C.V.
Bajo el sello editorial PAIDÓS M.R.
Avenida Presidente Masarik núm. 111, Piso 2
Colonia Polanco V Sección, Miguel Hidalgo
C.P. 11560, Ciudad de México
www.planetadelibros.com.mx
www.paidos.com.mx

First edition printed: October 2019
ISBN: 978-607-747-818-8

Total or partial reproduction of this book or its incorporation into a computer system or transmitted in any form or by any means is not permitted, whether electronic, mechanical, photocopying, recording or otherwise, without the prior permission writing from the copyright holders.

The violation of these rights may constitute an offense against intellectual property. (Arts. 229 and following of the Federal Copyright Law and Arts. 424 and following of the Penal Code.)

If you need a photocopy or scanning of some part of this work, please address at CeMPro. (Centro Mexicano de Protección y Fomento de los Derechos de Autor, http://www.cempro.org.mx.)

Printed in Litográfica Ingramex, S.A. de C.V.
Centeno núm. 162, colonia Granjas Esmeralda, Ciudad de México
Printed and made in Mexico - *Impreso y hecho en México*

To my followers, source of inspiration

CONTENT

1

THE
PILLARS OF WEALTH

—

I have been obsessed with spreading knowledge using the best possible teaching method so that people appropriate it and transform their daily reality. This book will be no exception and I will use all the teaching ability I have to make this reading experience life-transforming. I gain nothing by talking about wealth, education, financial freedom, inspiration, and about finding a transcendental meaning in the desire to be rich if I don't share ideas about how to achieve it. So setting the bar high from the beginning is not frightening.

I start from the certainty that each one of us is capable of becoming the person he/she wants to be. But this, as we will see throughout these pages, requires more than a powerful determination to do so. One of the most fascinating qualities that human beings have is their extraordinary ability to change and to always be able to improve. Saying that a transformation is not possible or that defects will be there forever because "we were born that way" is, from my point of view, a statement of mediocrity.

Over more than twenty years as an investor, coach, and financial analyst, people have repeatedly told me: "I want to make money but have failed to do so. It doesn't seem possible yet." I have been able to conclude through my own experience and that of many people that the more you look

for something with a selfish spirit, the more elusive and difficult to obtain it becomes. Today it is clear to me that it is imperative to have a deep motivation that could be the engine
to give these aspirations a transcendental meaning which
will lead us to discover the potential we have to overcome
any obstacle. Money, wealth, and abundance will come by
themselves, but only if we have carefully defined the reason
why we are seeking them.

It may sound simplistic, but defining this "life purpose"
requires going through some steps and shouldn't be con-
fused with the result expected from certain actions in life.
We will clarify the meaning of this in the following pages
through examples in the hope that all of those who discover
their "reason why" will feel the way what we have called "a
purple way of life" springs up and makes them different
from the ordinary person. You will also discover that there is
within you an unbeatable ability to supercharge, to become
so passionate about your "reason why" that you do achieve
what you propose. It is enough for now to note that from our
perspective, obtaining wealth, prosperity, and abundance is
directly linked to the growth of each individual as a person.
Give a hug, be kind and generous, call someone who may
not be expecting it, be firm, always aspire to more, and you
will realize how all of this is related to money.

People gain nothing by saying "I want to make progress financially" if their habits, if what they study, if what
they read, if what they participate in, and if the people they
surround themselves with always remain the same. And,
indeed, the same is true if their hours of sleep continue to be
long and placid while they wait for reality to change by itself
as if it were by magic. That is why I can say that there is no

difference between a person who is poor and a person who wants to be rich but does nothing useful to make it happen.

Arriving at these observations has been the fruit of my experience. I turned what for many is a tragedy into the opportunity of my life: being fired. I have repeated this in my lectures and seminars, and I reaffirm it every day. It was then that I faced myself, saw what I was made of, and found my lodestar. I changed my mindset and that made it possible for me to go from earning 800 dollars monthly as a university professor and researcher to earning a higher monthly income than any president or CEO of a private company in the region only four years later.

By the age of 35, I had been a professor, author of five books, and contributor for important economic journals in my country. I had also accumulated very valuable experiences in various entities in the private financial sector until that one defining moment arrived. So I developed the first seminar on investing over the Internet for non-experts in Colombia in 2000 when the vast majority did not have a computer and few even dared to make payments over the Internet. Currently, there are now more than 75 versions of this seminar.

In 2004, I founded Invertir Mejor (Invest Better) in order to make investing through the Internet accessible to all. Today, Invertir Mejor has achieved this goal in more than forty countries in which we have clients. However, what is even more important is that our purpose is no longer limited to investments; it is to inspire the lives of our partners and followers through a better financial education and personal growth. I am interested in inspiring millions of people and changing the way they live through my influence. I wanted

Invertir Mejor to become a cause rather than just a company. We have been succeeding at that thanks to the work of the committed team of people who I am very grateful for and to my wife, Alicia.

I think that the Universe evaluates us every day and the more determination you have, the more merit you accumulate. This determination, these desires, this passion that you impress on your work is fertile ground for good fruit to be harvested from. At any given moment in life, the Universe takes a picture in which the exact condition you are in is registered, and it depends on you to make sure that the picture is pretty and you are seen the way you want to be. This is what happened to me: I transformed what seemed to be an adverse situation into what, today, is my deepest reason for existing and what I dedicate 100% of my working hours to: teaching, inspiring, and *investing* in making people happier. As we will see, the less selfish and individual your "reason why" is, the more prosperity the Universe will return to you, and what would be better than to have it accompanied by money? Let's make it clear from the beginning, money itself is not the purpose. It is one of the desirable outcomes of a purpose that is strongly rooted in our being.

The secret is to BE in order to have; not to have in order to BE. Increase your inner richness, and you'll increase your outer wealth.

I have highlighted the word *invest* intentionally. When you invest funds, hopefully they will go into a business where that for which you came into the world, this transcendent proposal, which we have baptized as the "reason why" is deployed. This proposal should be related to what you do best with your talents and that is why you have to monetize it or turn it into money.

All human beings have defects—there is no doubt about that—but at the same time they have a plethora of abilities and skills that are only discovered during the most difficult times, and that they would not have believed possible to use before that. All of us, without exception, have talents. The difference is in who discovers them and converts them into something profitable. The majority of people underestimate that latent capital that they have, and learning to exploit it is also financial education as we will see in this book.

I have mentioned one of the determining factors in my career. It was one of them that led me to change my life and showed me a turning point where I could discover and enhance the talents I already had: having been fired. This situation confronted me and led me down a path toward the generation of new and higher income, a trajectory I want every reader to forge as well. The photo that the Universe took of me at that moment was a picture of a person facing a new and unexpected obstacle but endowed by nature with the determination to change the situation completely and turn it around in his favor.

I reached the point where I could corroborate that a "person's reality is based on what he believes is possible. Nothing will change until that person's reality changes and that only becomes reality when the person is capable of conquering himself, conquering his fears, and conquering his defects." I found myself forced to reflect deeply about my own talents and aspirations in order to convert that adversity into terrain where I could sow the seeds of my own destiny and transform that crisis into an opportunity. The questions that I faced were neither simple nor trivial: Why had I come into the world? What is it that I do best?

I didn't find the answers to them immediately. But when I looked at what I had been doing up to that time, I realized that the purpose of my life was to teach and inspire. To do those two things, I had talents such as the ability to speak in public, study, and be disciplined that would help me to do them well. The Universe was showing me that first picture was beginning to change, other paths were opening up, and the next photo was going to be radically different.

Just as I discovered and valued my talents and virtues, my defects were also still there and flourished to such an extent that they obscured what I was beginning to build. Success in my field of work had made me a person who was so, overbearing, and convinced that I possessed the absolute truth that not even I could stand myself sometimes. I lacked emotional intelligence and spirituality, and I literally humbled myself and overcame myself to acquire them.

I think that when you take success for granted, think it will always be there and that your capabilities can eclipse other things that are as important in life as how best to treat others, not losing control, and being more human, you are lost. I had succeeded in generating much more income than I had when I was employed. That was great. However, I gained nothing by treating people badly and not growing inwardly.

There was a catalyst in my life that showed me, as if in a revelation, that in order to be truly rich and prosperous, I had to change the way I was and the way I related to others.

It happened after I called a call center. As a result of the delay in their response time and service, I vented all of my anger on the person who was available on the other end of the line to deal with what I needed. It wasn't the first time. When I hung up, engulfed in my wrath, I went through a confrontation with myself that was surreal. I felt as if there was another presence in front of me that asked me what made me think I had the right to abuse another person and, at that moment, all defects that I wanted to eradicate began to emerge. Remember: I am convinced that human beings can be whoever they want and always become a better version of that.

It's not always an overnight process. But the first step is to determine that there has to be a change and, in my case, it had to be deep and radical. It had to be an authentic quantum leap that would take me from the point where I was, not to the next level, but much further and always beyond expectations.

That is how I made the decision to make that leap, to demonstrate to myself and those around me that I could become a better person. I decided to subject myself to one of the most difficult tests for someone who was proud and overbearing like I was. By means of coaching experiences in Neurolinguistic Programming (NLP) and personal growth exercises, I lived times when I felt very uncomfortable, exposed, and forced to serve others with humility and dedication. I had to conquer the pride that characterized me and the arrogance that closed doors; in other words, conquer myself. No book or course could match the experience itself of having put myself in other people's shoes without judging them, and thanks to that, correct some behaviors that were distorting my reality and hence blocking the true path to a prosperous life in every sense. Since this happened, the Universe has done nothing but send blessings although I know that there still are and will be many more things to correct. One should never put aside the determination and conviction that rather than changing step by step as we have always been told, it is possible to change rapidly if we put our minds to it. It is perfectly viable to be one person on Friday and be a different one the following Monday.

Why walk if you can fly; why proceed step by step if there are quantum jumps. Be careful with what you have gotten accustomed to live with.

Nothing will change until we change our reality. The invitation is to do something that we are afraid to do every day, travel, meet new people, read something different, run risks, and every day, go beyond that comfort zone in which nobody becomes great. The Universe will take each picture thus registering the merits of each moment and the determination with which you forge your character. All of that will add up and confirm that it is no coincidence that those who grow as people increase their income by proportions that they hadn't even imagined.

And if this level of prosperity and abundance comes into your life, the one that I want for you now and I know you will achieve, don't let yourself be deceived by those who cling to the old saying that you have barely 15 minutes of "fame and fortune" that you should take advantage of. When you achieve abundance and wealth, you will attract more if you are *leveraging* from a "reason why" that is solid, transcendent and has lasting effects. We will talk later about what the concept of leveraging means to me and to a purple person.

For the time being, if we agree then that we have to change habits and mindset in order to see a new reality, I think we will have started from a useful point. Abundance comes into your life once it is in your head. But this is intimately related to another fundamental aspect that I also had to be aware of and that is widely shared: language.

Abundance will be possible only when you change *the words you use daily*—not just the words you use to communicate with others but also the words you say to yourself. In other words, many words should be completely eliminated from your everyday vocabulary and from the way you talk to and about yourself both mentally and with others regarding your purpose, projects, goals, and desires.

Words are not carried away by the wind; words define your reality. Pay attention to the words you say, and to the words said to you!

Neurolinguistic Programming (NLP) is a tool that I absolutely recommend that will help you understand the great power that words have to attract wealth and abundance. When speaking to all the people who have attended my lectures and seminars, clients that I work with in Invertir Mejor, and my readers, I recommend going through the experience of participating in a PNL workshop or seminar at least once in their lives. Currently, this is widely available in all the countries in our region where you can do that. The major contribution of this experience is the development of an assertive and constant use of the words that articulate our desires and decree the fulfillment of our aspirations all the time on a daily basis. No one can do this for us. Decreeing what our "reason why" is, affirming our purpose in life, vanquishing conformity, and generating a prosperous reality for ourselves and our environment cannot be delegated or delayed. You will see that is even possible to walk on fire without burning yourself if you purpose to do it and repeat it to yourself just like I have done on multiple occasions.

At this point we can ask ourselves: if every human has the will power, the ability to change, and ways to use words more assertively and forcefully, why isn't everyone rich if the great majority want to be? There are several things that explain that. First of all, there are people who, having time and health to create wealth, don't do it by virtue of the fact that they are used to having everything handed to them and not having to make any effort. They spend their lives complaining, crying, lamenting, demanding subsidies and perks, and never develop everything they have within themselves or the infinite potential they possess basically because they have never been faced with true emergencies.

Only high pressure transforms coal into diamonds. It's sad to realize that the majority of people just die as coal because of fear of pressure, fear of facing true emergencies.

Urgency is the key. If you don't have it, create it. This is the way to find out what your true motivations are and discover why you came into this world. Ten percent of the people earn 90% of the world's income. That said, if you really want to be within that minority—which is a genuine aspiration—subject yourself to necessities, in other words, to extremes that will push you to develop your talents, work on your defects, and seek new or additional income. You must create the circumstances that will put pressure on your life or push you away from or pull you out of your comfort zone where you won't grow as a person. My invitation is to raise the bar higher every day; give yourself more ambitious goals every day. Leave home if that allows you to demand more of yourself, overdraw your bank account, travel without a dollar in your pocket, quit your job if you don't enjoy it, but please: do something that puts you on the ropes, let your genius flourish and see what you are made of if you want to fly and not just walk!

Focusing on pressing needs and motivated by your "reason why" or deepest motivation will generate financial habits that will define the future of your equity. Hence the "reason why" cannot be weak. You must communicate passion when you talk to people about this, and when you repeat it to yourself. Without determination or a reason for being in this world, you will never be rich. Without a motivation or urgent need that forces you to seek and generate income, you won't be rich either. And without habits or financial education, you won't meet your goal nor develop criteria and you will continue to invest in the same things as always.

One of the reasons why there are people who are poor and it is certain there will continue to be is that they keep accumulating more and more poorly used hours. That is poverty: a total sum of misused hours. When we have bad habits that don't contribute to the purpose that we are seeking, we are undoubtedly making poor use of time. Indeed, I think that sleeping more than six hours to be a necessity but nonetheless, unfortunate for attracting wealth. If God wanted one to sleep a lot, He would have already sent you death. If you have realized that you need money, you have to find out how to get it. Now ask yourself what habits you have that are needed to nurture that increase in financial capital and which ones you should abandon. If the Universe were to take a picture of your life at this point in time, what would that picture look like? Think of the things, people, and attitudes that would disfigure this picture and which ones you think should appear the next time this moment is captured. If it isn't clear, I hope this book and my videos, which are available on YouTube and online (Invertir Mejor), can help you with this.

2

TOWARDS A PURPLE LIFE

—

Being rich implies developing something special and extraordinary that will set you apart from other people. Something unique that will set you apart and that arises from a series of qualities and talents that you yourself have maximized. It's not a question of being different in appearance or superficially but rather of something deep within you. If you are one of those people who believe that they have no talents and cannot inspire others, I am going to show you that you may be wrong since all of us, without exception, have the raw material to always be better than we are.

My "reason why," my own motivation in life is to help you to start this process of discovery that will lead each of you to find your own motivation, one that is so strong, deep, sustainable, and transcendental that it will steer you towards paths of wealth and material prosperity. The most important thing for me is to guide each reader in the search for a purple process so that things and changes happen to them that generate wealth in their lives.

Many people have approached me and and told me with absolute certainty that they don't have any special talent that would give them even the slightest chance of becoming rich. As we will see, all of us have a plethora of talents to develop and monetize, i.e., to turn into money. Part of the key to generating income is in the latter. But, if from the start, someone thinks that he doesn't have any talent or something that makes him different or unique deep within his being, he is annulling the possibility of generating wealth with his thoughts and language. Thought and language are the most powerful things that we have for changing our reality positively, but if we don't handle them well, they become the most lethal weapons against our aspirations and dreams.

There are those who claim that the obstacle to becoming rich that they face is that they weren't born into a privileged family context in which they could dedicate themselves to what they really liked. As the saying goes, "they weren't born with a silver spoon in their mouths" and they point to their parents, their family, and their education as the factors that determined and condemned them to poverty for the rest of their lives.

I have also encountered those who believe that the problem lies in the place where they were born: countries without equal opportunity for everyone, meager resources, or closed social circles. They were so limited that they did not have the opportunity to make the connections they needed to reach prominent positions or be successful with their business ideas.

Some would say that they haven't been able to be successful because they aren't tall, attractive, slim, sexy, or whatever enough, or because they lack some quality that they believe would give them an advantage over others. They are able to enumerate a litany of excuses like an unending spiral, like a cycle of pretexts that never comes to an end, and that culminates in abolishing change and progress from their lives. Often, for example, women in particular feel that their gender places them at a disadvantage and there-fore they are condemned to never being rich, or not as rich as a man could be. I have proven that none of this is true. It is only a matter of limiting conversations that we carry on within ourselves and that everyone, without exception, can create the conditions for becoming rich. What is more, they should do so, but they need to overcome the fears and hang-ups that hold them back.

I won't deny anything as evident as the fact that every person is born into different circumstances, but, for me, that does not determine their destiny as if it were carved in stone and there were no remedy. On the contrary, I am a firm believer in the infinite possibilities that each person has to change their lives and always improve as we have already indicated. However, we will now add that making the decision *to be rich* has to do with taking control of your own life as a first step and assuming all of the responsibility for achieving that purpose without hiding behind the pretexts mentioned above.

In my talks and seminars, I constantly repeat the fact that the rich take responsibility for the results, not for the excuses. They don't blame anyone else for things not work-ing out or taking an unexpected twist. They take personal responsibility for the situation, participate actively in the process of creating wealth and, whatever the outcome, they always profit or learn at the end. The word failure isn't part of a purple dictionary. There is only experience, learning, and training, not failure. What is more, I always talk about how important it is to make the kinds of investments which you know ahead of time you are going to profit from, un-like what happens when you purchase a stock, a foreign currency, a commodity or a piece of land. Surely, as happens at these seminars, you are probably wondering: And what are these investments in which you know in advance you are going to make money? My answer is: when you invest in your "reason why". And the fact is, there is nothing more profitable than investing in what you do best, what you undertake passionately, what you are motivated to do, and what fulfills your purpose in life. And when I say profitable, I'm not just referring to money. It goes beyond that: it is the satisfaction that it contributes to what you came into the world to do.

Raise your income to the level of your dreams, or you'll see your dreams fall to the level of your income.

Let us remember that the Universe takes pictures of us: Ask yourself right now how much in control of your own life you are. How many excuses do you give yourself daily for not changing? Do you think that money itself is bad? Are you fully satisfied with your life just as it is today? What pretexts do you repeat to yourself to avoid dedicating 100% of your time to investing your material and emotional resources into what makes you different from others? Who is the only one who is responsible for what happens in your life? Do you, perhaps, blame others for what happens to you or for your failure to achieve what you set out to do? Finally, imagine what that picture would be like. Is it satisfactory to you, and do you feel happy and fulfilled with what you see?

A person who is always taking refuge in others, hiding, making excuses, or blaming everyone else for the bad luck they have had in life will never be rich or make progress. If this person is constantly looking for the solution to his own problems in others or if he continuously thinks that someone else's actions will harm him, it is his own defeatist mindset which is holding back any desire he has to become an extraordinary being and one who deserves wealth.

Along with these people there are also those who are comfortable with the situation they are in, those who don't want to change anything for fear of losing what little they have achieved and foolishly believing that they have reached the highest point they can. There are the people who, for fear of losing a job which allows them to receive a fixed salary every month, put off or bury forever their desires to earn more money and have the means to do certain things. These people are the ones who conform and, under a cloak of tranquility and parsimony, are resigned to the life they are living.

If you want to forego wealth, be a wealth repellent, and settle for what you have today, for that salary, for that comfort zone that, like a cancer, eats you up as you wait for the day that you begin to receive a pension when it comes (if it does come), you may find that you don't have enough vigor to enjoy it.

The comfort zone can give you security but not wealth. It can give you reassurance but not progress. Avoid it.

The comfort zone is a danger: there are people who are content with what they have, but their house is falling down, their children are studying in poor, mediocre schools and, out of necessity, they go to the same place as usual for vacation. Then they say: "I don't lack anything"; I ask them: What do you have too much of? It's not a matter of "I don't lack anything," since you can be satisfied through multiple ways in life. The issue doesn't lie in whether or not you are fulfilled, or if your life is full or not, but rather *how* it was satisfied or *how* you made your life a truly purple and satisfactory one. I want to stress that all of us always, always, always have the chance to choose, be free, and forge our destiny. We don't talk about *financial freedom* in vain.

Last of all, we cannot fail to mention those people who even criticize the fact of being rich and the taste for money per se. They approach the rich with suspicion or distrust, envy, antipathy and resentment. "There they go, those rich people; who knows where they are getting their money," or offensive comments which only show that they are unable to occupy themselves with their own life and deal with their own material and spiritual poverty. For example, I am convinced that, deep in their hearts, those who always criticize material things actually yearn for them, but don't have the courage to try to get them.

We also encounter people who, using phrases that are very deeply rooted in our Latin American cultures such as "less is more," "money is a problem," and "the one who needs the least is rich," cut off any initiative a person might have to change or make a quantum leap towards habits that would lead to prosperity and abundance at the root. They eliminate the essential and *legitimate* possibility that every human being has to desire to be rich, to find their "purple being" and effectively achieve levels of monetary income that are much higher than average and that they may not have imagined before.

Other sentences that abound are along the line of, "it's better to have friends than money" or "I prefer spiritual to material wealth." A purple person shouts from the rooftops: "I prefer both things! Friends and wealth; material and spiritual wealth," just as we don't want to choose between having hands or having feet. One must choose both things in life. Is it better to have friends than money? No, definitely not. I'm going after everything, I'm in a super-charged mode, and I haven't yet achieved even 1% of what I know I can achieve! That's the way I suggest you think.

Don't pick your friends by the amount of money they have. But please, not everyone has to be poor!

One of the ways to attract wealth is to think and say: "Wealth, I like you; richness, you fascinate me; come, sit at my table." But if I begin with hypocrisy, hiding myself and criticizing that which is material because it supposedly separates me from God, then I won't attract it. What I want is for us to step into the fire, make good use of our abilities and help people with all the determination we have rather than simply dedicating ourselves to berating ourselves over what we don't have or how unfair life may have been. Life is what it is. Things just happen. The importance of this phenomenon lies not in what happens, but in how we interpret what happens or the meaning we give it.

If anyone has a genuine desire to change their life, improve it, and generate wealth for themselves and for those around them, they must begin by reconfiguring the way they see the circumstances around them and how they talk about them. It's not a question of avoiding reality, but rather of developing one that makes it possible to work towards meeting one's goals and satisfying a deep and motivating "reason why."

A person who always sees the world as a permanent obstacle to achieving any goal, whatever it may be (not necessarily getting money), sees things differently than someone who has made it his purpose to achieve great things sees them. For example, it is one thing to say "someone hurt me, abandoned me, robbed me" or "that person took advantage of me" and another to speak of experiences as apprenticeships or opportunities that life placed in your path in order for you to learn something. Therefore, who doesn't make progress is always bemoaning life and asking "why me!" while a purple person or, in other words, someone who has launched out without fear into the conquest of wealth and abundance, always asks himself *what is the purpose behind what* happened to me and sees opportunities where only adversity appears to be. A person who's not purple would say, "They fired me from my job" while someone who is purple would assert, "I was laid off from my job to find my lodestar and know what I'm made of." Complaining may be human, but adapting is essential.

The above is part of a fundamental concept on which I base my conferences and sessions with my clients: the idea of *leverage*. We can say that the "why" turns us into victims while the "reason why" opens doors for us. In financial terminology, leverage has to do with going into debt, getting funds through loans in order to do something: for example, getting a loan to have working capital. That is leveraging in the traditional sense. I've given this word a spin in order to refer to *leveraging* as that quality of taking advantage of things that, in principle, would be impossible to take advantage of, such as an illness, being fired, a separation, an economic loss, or a bankruptcy. Those who develop a strong-willed attitude, who leverage life by taking advantage of everything that happens to them—even things which would not appear to be susceptible to being used—radiate a different and powerful individual energy. Their determination to be different and make progress is the seed of their success.

We have already said that 10% of the people in the world earn 90% of the world's income. That said, if you really want to be within that minority, an aspiration which is genuine, you have to begin to differentiate yourself from others. In a world like the current one in which everyone wants to be like others in order to seem "normal," the greatest achievement that one can have is to be oneself. When you are and express what you feel, there are people that will be bothered by that. However, you shouldn't consider people like that important. The people that you really are important to should not be bothered by the fact that you're developing as a person and triumphing, and that you are and express what you are.

What's the problem with leading a "normal life"? That your income will be normal! What's normal is forgetable; purple is remembered.

Just as you should seek to differentiate yourself as a person, don't be afraid to see yourself as a product. You as a person are one, and as such must differentiate yourself. If you don't differentiate yourself from the rest because you act like everyone else, dress like everyone else, watch what everyone else watches, listen to what everyone else listens to, talk about what everyone else talks about, you will turn into a commodity, an essential good, a raw material, and be accordingly paid poorly.

First of all, let's start from the fact that people who develop the habits of the rich and are financially free don't depend on a salary. Second, they generate income through business and investments; and, third, they are unique, non-replaceable. Generating an income that is an addition to a salary is absolutely necessary for this process and to get it, they have to leave behind the fears that tie them to the apparent security and tranquility of the comfort zone. Subjecting yourself to pressing needs and setting high and ambitious goals for yourself will make you push yourself harder and show you what you're really made of. It will bring out the diamond you have inside. When you discover what puts fire in your belly, the thing that really charges you up more all the time, you'll have found your talent.

How can you know if you are a commodity or if you really are a product that will make a difference? Do the following exercise, for example. After a conversation with someone, reflect: How have you affected that person who you have been talking to? What difference did you make, what did you contribute to him? What did you teach him? How did you transform him? Do you think that your conversation is desirable for that other person? Do you talk about the same things everyone else does, or complain, or do you separate from the herd and pass along your energy?

When a wonderful product stands out from the competition, everyone is going to choose it. The same thing happens with people. Some are capable of leaving the flock and, with their persistence and tenacity, they manage to stand out from the crowd: the first step in attracting wealth. How can we differentiate ourselves then? The first thing is to touch the heart and awaken emotions. There is nothing more addictive than emotions, sexiness, sensuality, than what is interesting, what is striking. Ask yourself how passionate you get when you get involved in a conversation, when you make a presentation, when you greet someone, or when you simply sit down some place so that others look at you. You are not what you do, you are what you cause. Passion is contagious, but you can only be passionate when there is a sufficiently powerful purpose in life to draw forth that energy—a solid and sincere "reason why." Being purple, which is synonymous with being extraordinary—a different person—is not accumulating money just because. Being purple is developing that which I came into this world to do, benefiting thousands, millions, and making them happier: Eureka, that's the way money comes in!

Have an impact on millions and you will be filled up with millions.

From the moment you introduce yourself, the instant when you open your mouth and talk to other people about yourself and what you do, how you shake hands, how you look, how you dress, how you smile or not, how fast or slow you walk; all of the signals your body gives are essential for you to sell yourself to the world. Seven percent of our language is words, 38% is the tone of voice, and 55% is physiology—how you move your hands, shoulders, eyes. All of that speaks for you. The gestures and words that you use with others will make you a needed, indispensable product or one that doesn't interest anyone. What would you rather be?

You may have possibly responded that you wanted to be a product that was different, desirable, unique, and highly valued and even better, one that produces earnings in money. It isn't enough to simply want it, however. You need to decree it, and this means to say with complete confidence that you really will become that but not in a year, in months, or days but rather *starting right now.*

Your language has to be assertive outwardly with others and also inwardly, in the words you use to talk to yourself. The language we use to talk to ourselves in our daily life, the way we articulate what we are *going to* achieve and not simply what we desire makes a big difference between the purple people and the rest.

Just remind anybody who tries to stand in your way as you seek to be happy: My happiness is not negotiable!

Let's do an exercise. Someone may say: "I want to visit Europe with my family some day." That's not bad—the intention is good. But note the radical difference if this same person decreed his purpose this way: "I will travel in first class around Europe with my family in July of next year, and we will have the best vacation that we have ever dreamed of." Words are very powerful and we make will them a reality only if we rely on them to affirm our purposes.

It is imperative to always send messages of abundance assertively to both ourselves and others while eliminating words that sow doubts, increase fear, or curb our action. This is key in the generation of wealth. I regret having come to this topic so late in my life, but I have arrived, and now I can share its importance with you.

In my case, neuro-linguistic programming was an exceptional tool for clarifying my language and becoming conscious of the fact that the way I articulated what I intended had an indirect influence on whether these things were fulfilled or not. It also influenced the way I was perceiving reality. I discovered that, just as you do, I had an inner voice that put restrictions on my actions and constantly sabotaged my own life. I baptized that harmful, "toxic" voice and gave it a name: Matilda. It was a name that was chosen at random, but it helped me in that every time it invaded my thoughts with its pessimism, I could silence it and master it. "Matilda" was also the name for my fears that hindered me and didn't allow me to act, since they were so strong that they paralyzed me at times. That voice is the one that, in the face of crises, repeats that all is lost. It's the voice that says not to give up the security of receiving a salary at the end of the month because without it we will die of starvation. It is the voice that says "you are not able to do this or that," the voice of blame and resignation, the voice that cries, "don't do that because of what they will say about you." It is the voice that says "stand still, don't take risks because you may fail".

All of us have an inner voice like Matilda, and we have to silence her if we have truly decreed that we will be rich in our lifetimes. I know that right now you are thinking: And how do I silence it? When we become greater as people, that voice gets tired of competing. When we have high ideals, strong motivations, Level 10 as I call them, a compelling reason why that consults our strengths and tastes, the demands we make of ourselves will be so great, the challenge to excel will be so vigorous that Matilda will become increasingly smaller.

Let's return for a moment to the process of discovering personal talents. Let's assume that you have reflected on everything which makes you different from others, those talents that only you have and that turn you into a wonderful and essential product for this world. What good does it do if you don't show it, if no one knows that it exists? How many people do you reach with your talent; how many do you inspire with your talent? If the answer is "no one" or "very few" or "I don't know," that is the reason for the limited money that you currently have. This is why your financial situation is poor. Many businesses fail and so do many entrepreneurs because they disregard this truth. At the beginning, these people sell their products to friends and family who are happy to buy them in order to support this new idea, this illusion; but after that? There is no more market, and they don't have anyone to sell to.

This leads us to conclude that to be rich, it is essential that you communicate that talent to as many people as possible. Build on technology. This was what the Internet was made for, and that is its great power. It can reach many people even while you are sleeping, since technology exists to do what you do without having to be physically present. Give your talent freely; don't skimp on it.

If you have a business, what are you waiting for to have it online? If you know how to do something that others don't, why don't you advertise it? Don't underestimate your talent. Don't underestimate your abilities. There are thousands of human beings in the world who need them. Show what you do and promise. Don't write so much— demonstrate, demonstrate. If you have a product, display it. If you sell, distribute, or are successful at a service, show the testimonies about this service. Have no doubt about it; all of that will bring more money at the same time as it makes many more people happy and multiplies the effects of your endeavor on life. Being purple isn't accumulating money; it is also contributing to the happiness of people. Investing in this is investing in yourself while investing in others.

While you keep on thinking that selling is not for you, your income will be limited. Even without doing anything you are already selling yourself.

To summarize what we have stated up to now, being purple is the result of a personal decision to take responsibility for our own destiny, to make use of the talents that we have for our own benefit and for the happiness of others, to see ourselves as a product and lean on the transforming power of language. Seth Godin, author of several books on marketing, wrote a very important one concerning purple cows. In essence, he said the following: You're strolling along a field path and suddenly you see a lot of cows. Most of them are black and white, as expected, and you initially think: "Such beautiful cows"! You continue walking and the black and white cows are becoming part of the landscape, all the same. The view gets boring. But then something catches your attention again! What is it? An extraordinary cow appears, different from all the others: a purple cow.

The lesson from this metaphor is that normal is boring, and that it is essential to become different. However, I go a step further: for me, normal stinks. It produces no money, is quickly forgotten, and only the personal decision to change that situation will make the emergence of extraordinary things possible. I see the white cows as an incentive to be more purple. The purple cows don't complain, the purple cows leverage, a purple cow leaves a message, and gets people talking. If only wealth were important, then all of the rich would be purple, but they are not. How many are there who get fat behind a desk, who line their pockets, and no one learns anything from them. I don't want a life like that. It isn't a purple one. I'm not interested in just accumulating. I'm not only interested in you becoming rich. If you become rich without becoming a better human being, that's not purple. It isn't extraordinary. I want you to have an impact,

to transcend, to have an influence. I would like you to accumulate wealth, but only as the effect of the reason why
you came into this world. As the late Wayne Dyer famously
wrote, you don't concentrate on the result. Concentrate on
your life purpose and that purpose will take you to the result.
In sessions with Invertir Mejor VIP partners, the fact that
many of them believed that their reason why is to be rich,
have financial freedom, have much more free time available,
or travel around the world drew my attention. This isn't a
"reason why", I tell them; it is only the logical consequence
of developing one. If you only concentrate on a personal
benefit without thinking of others, without serving or without helping, the scope of your progress will be very limited.
Blessings come in unimaginable proportions when we give
our purpose in life a meaning that turns it into an obsession
based on which it will end up benefiting millions of people.

3

QUANTUM JUMPS: FORGET STEP-BY-STEP PROGRESS

———

In my talks and sessions I have with my Invertir Mejor partners, I put a lot of emphasis on the need to develop a greater and more transcendent purpose in life as a requirement for being rich. I'll never tire of repeating that being rich isn't limited to accumulating money nor is it a synonym of strengthening our bank accounts. It is only the logical consequence of having habits of prosperity, a mindset focused on growing as people, and the ability to monetize the talents that we all have. We will achieve this if we conquer our fears, and it will be feasible to do so if we take quantum leaps in our lives.

The idea that goals are reached "step by step" is very widespread in our culture, and therefore, we should wait until the personal and external conditions are generated for our dreams to come true. This way of thinking does not coincide with the mindset of those who have habits of wealth. As I have stated: "step by step" would go a long way if we were to live 500 years. Being a rich person is not synonymous with scrimping and placidity. We tend to think that the rich are relaxed, sunbathing next to a swimming pool, enjoying a cocktail, or playing golf because they already have everything and have reached their goals. This isn't the case. They seem to be relaxed precisely because even though they are looking for more and have goals that are increasingly ambitious, they know where to go to generate the higher income that will allow them to get the things they want. In addition, they are focused on their next goal and on their purpose in life. They can continue to generate income even while they are sleeping because their determination is so powerful that it has forced them to maximize their qualities, and because, for a long time, they have known that generating income shouldn't always require their physical presence.

What opposes the "step by step" culture? It would be the deep conviction that it is possible to leap from one level to another and, not simply to the next level, but rather to others that are increasingly beyond that given that developing the habits of the rich lies in finding ways of life that differentiate you from others and in turning away from the "step by step" and the widespread "let's-wait-and-see-what-happens" thinking which are virtually synonymous. If "step by step" has a slow and deliberate rhythm in which we go from 1 to 2 and from 2 to 3 and so on while waiting a long time between each step, it is likely that we will grow old still waiting for what we desire. As is popularly said, we could grow roots waiting for things to happen and when what we want arrives, we may not be able to enjoy it or it will be too late.

With respect to some colleagues who say: "buy luxuries at the end," it turns out that, in the end, when we are old and tired, we won't have the same vigor to enjoy what we have acquired nor the knees we need to walk around the house we have always yearned to have or the streets of that beautiful city that we have dreamed of visiting since we were children. Imagine yourself traveling to Europe with your loved ones, but you can't walk very far along the city streets or the eyesight you need to read a map is failing, or you can't eat anything while going through the stores in Barcelona where they sell ham because it has high cholesterol. It's too late. I didn't wait long to get what I had dreamed of because time was going by, and time doesn't return. The luxuries of life are purchased when you have the financial education to pay for them and the necessary vigor to enjoy them. If a 30- and a 70-year-old person each buy a million-dollar home, each will have paid a different price because each will enjoy it differently. The young man paid less, since he will enjoy it longer. That is why I say that the price of an asset is never the same for different people since that depends on the ability that each one has to enjoy it. When I buy a luxury car, travel first class, or get a brand-name watch, I make sure from the beginning, and even before the purchase, to enjoy, smell, feel, and touch what I am buying. From that point on, the purchase is well worth the money, or which is the same, the purchase begins to be profitable and justified.

As long as you don't taste caviar, you will continue to believe that the world is made of chicken. Go for the best!

I often speak about quantum jumps. This is the opposite of "step by step". I discovered in my own life that it was possible to go from 1 to 5 without having to go through 2, 3 and 4. And afterwards from 5 to 10 or 20 or 100, or whatever I set my mind to, but without delaying or disregarding the circumstances. Remember that a truly rich person is able to, first, take charge of his own life and take responsibility for it and the results; and second, reshape his own reality, see it differently, and build it based on seeing everything from a different angle—even the most terrible adversities and calamities. Therefore, if your deepest desire is to be rich and generate more money than what you earn now, prepare yourself to take quantum leaps and stop watching passively how the grass in your little garden, in the little plot you control, is growing right now. Because if you want to be rich—and I hope you do become rich—you have the whole world ahead to conquer.

Starting now, from the moment you read these lines, you should decree into your daily life that you are a rich person. I want you, starting right now, to visualize yourself as the person you want to be without waiting to become that person before you behave like it. On social networks I have repeated: "Picasso didn't wait to be Picasso before he began to behave like Picasso." Do not say that you will be rich in twenty or thirty years. Or that you should wait until you are what you want to be before you behave that way. Starting today, and treating it like something that cannot be delayed, repeat this great purpose to yourself. In order to fulfill it, how we see ourselves in the future and how we behave in the present are essential. Then, if you visualize yourself a certain way in the near future or in the medium term, from now on you should start the changes that will take you there immediately rather than "step by step." Quantum jumps are produced by extraordinary experiences, extraordinary people, extraordinary books, extraordinary trips; not by what is common which only keeps people on the "step by step" path.

When someone tells you that in life one makes progress step by step, ask him: "Do you know what a quantum jump is?"

There lies the major difference between a person with a poverty mindset and another person that develops the mindset of the rich. The first postpones and postpones both things, and changes his mind and waits however long it takes between step 1 and step 2 while setting no deadline. They may even take forever to take the first step. The second, on the other hand, lives in the present, doesn't procrastinate, and their natural state in life is urgency. Everything must come about as soon as possible because there is no time to lose. The rich always remember a phrase mentioned several times in this book: poverty is the sum of misused hours.

These pressing needs have to do with a theme that has stood out several times in my life, and in everyone's, since it is natural and human: death. I see death as a very interesting concept for redefining priorities and making progress faster. Think about death, about how you want to be remembered when you stop breathing, about what condition you want to be in when death comes with no warning. When we have unlimited time to do things, we adopt middle class thinking—let's go "step by step." But when we say "our days are numbered" or we have many friends and family members with terminal diseases around us, for example, we are faced with what the time we have in this world means. We cannot continue the "step by step" culture because the time we have to live isn't unlimited, and when you become aware of this, you will be concerned about making the quantum jumps, the abrupt leaps, rather than the typical gradual progress.

Once someone asked me about what had happened in my life that increased my income so quickly and notably. To answer the question, I thought about what really had happened and came to the conclusion that in order to have made a quantum leap in income, I must have completed something I have baptized a "quantum triangle." In the middle of the triangle is the person's purpose, his "reason why." The strengths are found at the upper angle, resources in time and money are at the left angle, and Level 10 motivation on the right angle. The essence is very simple: when your strengths, what you do best, relates to your "reason why," when time and money is invested in your "reason why," and when that "reason why" or life purpose is the thing that motivates you the most, the "quantum triangle" is complete and, I repeat, that is necessary for quantum jumps. However, let's look at what happens to most people.

First of all, they are not clear about what their "reason why" is and often confuse it with anything that is just something they like or do well. Second, they don't always use their strengths. It is no surprise then that you find an employee at a bank whose greatest strength is painting or a person who cleans windows on the highest floors of a building whose strength is writing. Third, since their purpose in life isn't clear, they waste the resources, time and money, they have by squandering them or dedicating them to third party causes. And last of all, their Level 10 motivation is to build a house for their mom, have free time, travel around the world, or get a lot of money—all of which are only the logical consequences of a well-developed life purpose. Now you see, my dear reader, the reason why "the majority die as coal having had everything they needed to die as a diamond."

Death is, then, a way to attract wealth in the sense that by having limited time, the feeling of urgency and pressure will increase. These conditions are necessary to make our genius flourish and for us to achieve unimaginable results. It is good for us to be conscious of that in order to make our changes in life much more rapidly and faster-paced, and for us to stop worshiping the "step by step" process that makes products in series, exactly the same, white cows rather than purple ones, average beings rather than extraordinary ones.

History only remembers extraordinary people, the obsessed and the intense. Normal people are quickly forgotten; there were too many of them.

How do you become extraordinary? How can you truly be purple? We have already given you several clues throughout these pages. The power of intention is invaluable and having taken the first step of determining and decreeing change in our lives is basic. We could say that the attitude alone does not cure cancer, but it does help us to cope with it better and even to get through the most complex stages.

Nevertheless, it is essential to activate engines so that the intention itself, the huge purpose that motivates us to seek greater material wealth is carried out. In other words, if our immense and transcendental purpose is fulfilled, it is because we have motivations that are so strong that we manage to overcome any fear that could limit our ability to achieve it. We have to overcome that inner voice that blocks us and contaminates our thinking with toxic and negative ideas. I have given these motivations a score and refer to them as "Level 10 motivations." A motivation that is strong and solid enough will nip any fear in the bud. We will see this through an exercise that you yourself can repeat.

Let's assume that 10 is the highest rating that can be granted and 1 the lowest. Our motivations should always be at 10 so that our defects and fears look small beside them. You may have a defect and a fear that, up until now, has sabotaged you. Don't worry about the fact that it exists. Get busy finding those big motivations that will eclipse them the same way I did. People frequently ask me if it scares me to talk about money issues publicly. I usually say the following: let's give that fear a score. Suppose your score is 7. What does it matter if the fear is 7 when my motivation is 10. If that "reason why" is a flame that doesn't go out; an inner fire that drives me with passion, that commits me to the word "serve," and makes me willing to give everything I have in order to fulfill it. We can continue to have flaws and fears. And a big motive is needed to compete with them, one that, in my opinion, should be our life purpose.

Your attitude has led you to discover your talents, those qualities that make you different from others and that make you stand out. Remember that all of us have talents, but we have to cultivate them every day, dedicate our strongest efforts to them, water them as if they were plants, take care of them. Invest your time and resources in them, in strengthening the strengths as I usually say it. If one of my talents, if one of my strengths is to express myself well in public, I cannot remain quiet. I have to speak out more strongly every day. As I read more, I know more words. When I am more spiritual, I send a more meaningful message. When I have more passion for what I talk about, I reach more hearts. That is what I do. I don't keep my mouth shut. Refusing to grow in what you do the best is a good way to stagnate, and whoever stagnates in our current days can be sure that he is moving backwards. Your proficiency doesn't stop, even though you reinvent yourself and reduce it.

So we have two definite ingredients: attitude and talents. But our fears and defects, many of which are fostered by our environment, walk alongside them. How do I overcome them?

Nothing gives me more pleasure during a personal session than being able to destroy somebody's fear of progress in less than a minute's time.

There are people who burn with passion. They are like lit torches. They have blood in their eye. They are full of energy. They are sharks that smell blood. Other people may feel like ice cubes: they are low in energy and with so many fears and defects that they eclipse their motivations and don't allow them to thrive. We can have fears, all of us have them. We can have defects, all of us have them, but if my motivation, my reasons for living, the causes I fight for are branded on me with a hot iron, what does it matter if the fears and defects pop up? Ideally, I would give them a score of 7 over 10 as I explained in a previous example. Level 10 motivations allow us to make quantum jumps. They aren't negotiable, and starting right now I want them to be the most important thing in your life.

Finding the Level 10 motivations has to do with beginning to speak differently, surrounding yourself with different people, beginning to embrace great prospects and objectives in life with winning words that will be fulfilled within a decreed and not very distant time. An immediate motivation can be, for example, something personal: "get ahead", "make progress in life", "be somebody", "I want to be a millionaire." I hear this frequently, but I have to say that, even though all of it is fine and dandy, it is still very vague and ethereal. It isn't anything that is really different in your life, because millions of people want the same thing. Your motivations should be the pillars that support your "reason why" and that will cause it to become a reality.

We agree that you should be different in order to be rich. And that in order to be different you have reflected deeply about what special talent you have that you can use economically. You have come up with something that is your potential winner. In my case, and as I have already mentioned, I realized that one of my strongest talents is to speak in public and teach people things about financial education and personal growth. But that's still not a motivation. The talent has to be turned into a motivation by finding a goal that gives meaning to the development of that talent. "I am going to teach millions of people to improve their financial habits by using my public speaking skills." This is a Level 10 motivation when I dedicate 100 % of my energy, resources, and time to it. At this point, you will ask about the "reason why." My "reason why" is for these millions of people to reach levels of economic well-being and happiness they had not achieved before.

> **When someone has Level 10 motivations you'll notice it in their eyes. When they talk about them, you'll notice that person going into a supercharged mode.**

The few things I know how to do well, I do all day. You can never, never stop doing what you do best. You will never be yourself if you don't dedicate yourself to doing what you do best. The key is for your strengths to have an intimate relationship with your "reason why" (the upper angle of the quantum triangle); for them to go forward together and feed each other. It is easier for me to teach and inspire if I speak the way I am speaking. I know that that is a strength, and I water that plant daily. Here is another key which I emphasize in order to get money: whatever you are strong in, make it stronger every day. When we have a specific, clear life purpose, we invest in it, dedicate time to it. That way, we will be devoting our energy to that which we are strongest in, what we are passionate about, what we do well, and above all, that which we came into the world to do. And the other, motivation 10: Level 10 motivation should be there to develop my "reason why." A pure quantum triangle.

Let's analyze a real example. A partner in Invertir Mejor told me: "My main motivation is my daughter." Well, that's not bad, but could she be more specific, I told her. She thought about it and said it again: "My main motivation is for my daughter to lack nothing, to have an excellent education, and everything she needs." Much better, but something more is missing. This is a powerful motivation: your children, your family. But a Level 10 motivation doesn't consist of acquiring or ensuring that you have material things or material living conditions. It is creating new and happy realities for those we love.

Therefore, I advised this person, a single mother and businesswoman who has managed to set up and make her own business successful, to express her vision another way: "I will ensure that my daughter always has the education and quality of life necessary for an excellent, high-level intellectual, emotional and physical development and for her development as a good person." Note the affirmative language, "I will ensure," and the emphasis on what is material being for something higher, human, and for the service of others. It is a "reason why", a high and noble purpose.

"Juan Diego, the thing is I don't believe that I can achieve that so easily," she told me. I asked her why she believed that. Fortunately and thanks to her persistence, she already had the economic conditions on which to build greater wealth and achieve a higher income. She said: "It scares me." Naturally, what lay ahead of her was a huge challenge. There is no need to fear, I insisted. "I don't know if I can do it. Today education is very expensive, the world is very dangerous for children, and I have to work a lot now because of my new obligations and the business that I have started. I'm not sure." I saw that her fear was linked to a great insecurity.

"What is your greatest fear?" I asked. After a few seconds, she answered. "I am very insecure and I find it hard to make decisions. I have taken risks at times but I'm still very afraid to throw myself into the unknown." This fear wasn't a small thing but rather one that was deeply rooted and could prevent her from fulfilling her motivation. "I am also afraid of failure, afraid of what people will say, of losing money, taking on risks, so many things. Like anyone else, I am afraid of losing money most of all," repeated this person who had already achieved a number of successes over her lifetime. This fear seemed to have completely paralyzed and blinded her. When she spoke of this, her level 10 motivation (her daughter) dropped to second tier. The light that illuminated her eyes when she mentioned her little girl and how she visualized her in the future couldn't longer be seen.

As if it were in a set of scales, her indecision weighed more than her wonderful intention of making her daughter's life happy and extraordinary. I suggested that we make a deal, make a change that would remove her fear or at least make her see it differently. She couldn't refuse.

"Starting right now", I said, "from this very moment on, you are going to make a commitment with yourself that with respect to any decision of any type you have to make within the next month you will make it within one minute or you will never see your daughter again". I saw the change in her expression immediately. We were using a very powerful tool that we have already spoken of—language—to reshape a reality she took for granted, that of being an insecure person. What is more, a reality of someone possessed by insecurity and, thus, unable to take action on things. I wanted her to see reality differently and above all for the main motivation of her life, her daughter, to take the leading role so that her fear and insecurity would recede into the background. She limited herself to saying: "Of course I would be more re-solved and faster about making decisions in order to see my daughter again." And I told her: "And what happened to your indecision"? She was silent and stared at me. The defect was gone because a pressing need had appeared: see her little girl again.

On another occasion someone told me: "Juan Diego, I'm afraid of heights." I don't believe you. If your daughter called you for help from a high floor in a building that was on fire, would you climb up for her? "Of course!" And what happened to your fear of heights? "But this has to do with my daughter, Juan Diego."

One more example: "I have a very bad memory; I forget everything." I don't believe you. If a beautiful woman, one, by the way, you are enchanted with, gives you her telephone number so that you can call her next Friday, will you for-get it? "No, of course not." And what happened to your bad memory? "But it is a woman who fascinates me, Juan Diego."

I could continue with an endless list of examples but the moral or teaching is repeated: the fear or defect you have is not important. What's important is for you to have a Level 10 motivation to overcome them or eclipse them so that they don't matter.

Any unprepared person could say: "Juan Diego, the thing is, in the three examples that you gave, the person had to choose between their defect and something urgent or be-tween their fear and something urgent and therefore they had no choice. They had to act no matter what because, in the first case, she would not see her daughter again or, in the second, the daughter would die in the fire or, in the third case, he would lose the woman he liked." I ask: Do you mean there is something more urgent than our "reason why"? Nothing, from my point of view. Otherwise, what did we come into this world for? Fulfilling our life purpose is so urgent that there is no time at all to seriously think about or consider the flaws or fears that attempt to sabotage it. It is as simple as that.

Repeat this exercise on your own: make a list of motivations that support the purpose you came into this world for or what we have called the "reason why." If you aren't clear on this point, don't be alarmed. Think about your innate talents again and what you love to do. Along with your motivations, think about what the fears are that hinder you in your life. There doesn't have to be a fear related to each motivation. They can be general, and these are even more challenging to eradicate.

Why I came into the world: the reason for my existence and why I want to be rich		
Talents What makes me purple	**Level 10 motivations** What I fight for every day	**Fears** What restricts me and I must uproot from my life

Let's assume that an opportunity to invest in a business arises next month. There is the chance of winning or losing, of course. But if we place our Level 10 motivation beside this opportunity, we will be forced to profit. Losing stops being an option as long as the motivation is much stronger. We will do everything within our power to gain, and we will win since the mere possibility of not achieving a Level 10 motivation should be the engine to push aside all fear. Example: "If you don't invest in this business, you will never see the dearest person around you again." Put your goals in these types of terms: If I don't take the risk, I'll never have the house I deserve. If I don't step into the ring now, I may be forced to depend on a pension. Remember, you deserve to and can be rich. But to pressure yourself to reach that goal, you cannot postpone your motivations and let fear take control of you.

"Juan Diego, I fear risk, volatility, whatever isn't safe." I'm afraid of straight highways, because on those you're most likely to fall asleep.

You can have any defect you want, you can have all the fears you want, and multiply them by 100 if you want to. But what you should work on is having a motivation that is so brutally strong that defects and fear crouch down and hide under the table when they see motivation appearing. Literally speaking, I was afraid to walk on coals. And I did it. What could happen to me? Burn myself. But what was the motivation? When I reached the other side after having walked on fire, on coals that were at 800 °C with industrial alcohol added to make the flames climb higher, I was going to feel like Superman—"ready to conquer the world". If there's a huge reward, flaws and fear do not exist. So I did it. My mind was greater than the fear, the physical conditions, the fatigue. My determination and will made me forget about the pain and the possible blisters that I would have. This is a sample of the power of the mind and shows that we can achieve what we want.

The future is uncertain, of course; we all know this. But how can I act in the present to make that future better? By overcoming the fears that bind and limit me. Taking risks, or, as I say in my lectures, creating pressing needs will force you to fight for your motivations and goals. It will give transcendent meaning to your actions and call abundance into your life.

The great actors only became great when they took a step forward and took the risk of doing things differently from the rest of the people. Only when they put themselves in front of the floodlight that made them stand out from the others on the stage did they take a step beyond the comfort of the group and of anonymity. Take the step that you deem necessary to make yourself stand out. Don't let the white cows keep you at home among your friends or your colleagues. "Come, stay here, why take any risks?" they will ask you. "Crazy", they will say about you. But do it. Being rich implies seeing an opportunity before others see it, separating yourself from the flock, and conquering your fears the only way possible: by facing them and setting a huge competitor up beside them, a Level 10 motivation.

Your Level 10 motivation is not "saving humanity or saving the world." It's "saving the human beings who are suffering from cancer in the hospitals in my city." It is something more concrete and focused, for example. It is the first step to something bigger which will be followed by larger and larger motivations. You must think bigger without fear of failure and without sabotaging yourself. Create new pressing needs, new priorities every day. Have you helped someone yet? Well, help more people now. That's not enough? Then expand the effect of your action to more and more people and don't limit yourself.

These are the true quantum jumps. I am going to briefly give you five suggestions that have served me to that end and to find my "reason why."

First: find a purpose in life that is related to my strengths and that makes me stand out from others the most. That extraordinary quality or qualities that make me unique.

Second, that the motivation to develop that life purpose awakens such an appetite in me that I see the arrival of a Monday with the same joy that I feel when I see the arrival of a Friday.

Third, read a lot. If we don't read, we won't think of anything. Read books, magazines, articles, material on the Internet, anything, but at least, feed your imagination and ideas.

Fourth, become more spiritual. What does that mean? If you, for example, could connect yourself to a good cause or sponsor, to mention a few examples, the reintegration of street children or help at a geriatric hospital, if you could participate in a prayer group, or one for meditation, that would work magic. When you acquire a new spiritual dimension, when you see people differently, when you say that "there must be something good in that person" instead of judging them, you attract an infinite amount of positive things into your life.

And the fifth suggestion, but no less important is the following: We need more pressing needs in our life. Each one of you will decide whether or not to leave home, quit your job, travel without a single dollar in your pocket, or overdraw your account and spend more than you earn. There are people in the sessions to whom I have said: I need to see you overdrawn, and they look at me as if to say you have gone out of your mind! Yes, of course, they are in a comfort zone where nobody becomes great, as I have already said. When everything is absolutely measured and limited, life is mediocre and poor. You will never know what you're made of. Sometimes spending more than what we receive in a month is the perfect way to make ourselves conscious of the higher income we need to pay those expenses.

Don't keep postponing the luxuries you deserve. No one has promised you tomorrow.

Now, do you have a lot of money and lost your ambition? Be touched by altruism and donate it, and then, starting with limited capital you will develop the hunger you need again. The day that you conform to your life, the day your life enters the comfort zone, you will have become poor. Conformity is a dead cow in the middle of life—a smelly, unburied corpse. We need to have a purple purpose in life. The majority have average purposes and we don't want to be like the majority. One cannot be in the minority doing what the majority does. We need great, noble, irreverent purposes because we only have this life to enjoy, and what a shame if death should come before we have lived life the way we should have.

There is nothing more profitable than being happy. That is what we came into this world for—to be happy in what we do.

I know that all of us have a purple gene that distinguishes the one who is determined because I have seen it. You just have to let it act. One must have an inner fire, the motivation to do things. We all have an entrepreneur gene. In some of us, life has forced us to develop it, but others will die without having used it because they have been absorbed by a poorly paid job that they never enjoyed. It's not about being an entrepreneur or an employee. It's simply about either having a clear idea of your purpose or not.

That's the difference. There are people who prefer the "step by step" and comfort, but from now on I want you to make quantum jumps and live with a constant urge to generate new income.

4

GOING VIRAL: BECOMING RICH WITH SOCIAL NETWORKS

—

It makes no sense nowadays for the computer or phone you have in your home or office to be the most expensive and underutilized decoration you have. These devices which, like others, have revolutionized the lives of millions of people around the world, especially since the last decade of the 20th century and the first decade of the 21st century, should be used to the maximum to generate wealth and financial liberty.

Technology should work for human beings, and this is also true in the search for new sources of income. If you have a fixed salary at this time and are content with it, you will never be truly rich no matter how high that salary may be. Remember that we start from the fact that it is always possible to achieve more than you already have. It's imperative, as we will proceed to explain, to generate passive income, income that doesn't require your physical presence, and that you can procure while you sleep in order to live the life you want and not depend on a salary. Ask yourself, how much income apart from that salary do you have per month? When there is no passive income, it's because you're not leveraging well enough. And one of the reasons this occurs is because your business and ideas aren't on the Internet yet.

So your personal computer and your phone should be indispensable tools for generating. In addition, add to that the options that mobile devices such as tablets and iPads are providing for getting access to more sources of information and managing different transactions and business deals due to the data plan connections these devices have to Internet from anywhere.

Your entrepreneurial ingenuity, your will to be rich, your determination to change financial habits and to build a quality of life unlike the current one have an unequaled ally on the Internet. This has revolutionized the lives of people as did the emergence of the social networks, whether they be Facebook, Twitter, or Instagram, to name a few. We will talk about them in detail and, especially, about the way we can use them to help, serve, and generate income wholesale and to make authentic quantum jumps.

Digital technology and well-capitalized social networks will make it possible for you to maintain a constant stream of income even while you sleep, as I have already said, and thus achieve greater results with less effort, the true essence of leverage.

We have already talked about how discovering those unique talents that differentiate you from the rest turn out to be essential for beginning to prepare a path to economic prosperity. However, having talents does no good if no one knows about them, if they are not advertised. Social networks are the multiplying factor for that because, even though you may not believe it, there are thousands of people out there who are in need of what you produce, sell, distribute, think, or even what you have lived and experienced and want to share. When you understand what people need, or what people are crying out for, you will bring out better products with a higher profitability. The world is avid to know what we do to satisfy their needs; from how to make spaghetti to how to overcome the loss of a loved one, train a pet, change the oil in a car, or dance tango. We have thousands of possible ways to reach millions of people.

Imagine someone working for you 24 hours a day, helping you earn money without charging you. Who? Your YouTube videos. How many do you have?

But let's get back to a key question: What exactly does "generate passive income" mean? It means to discover and tap into the ways we currently have within our reach to avoid depending on a fixed salary, if we have one, or on income that comes from a single main activity. Essentially, "a passive income or, as it is also known, a residual income is income that goes into our pockets regularly due to an effort that we made once or made a few times but was enough to continue generating income for a long time." Examples: When I put a video on YouTube, I make a one-time effort, but it is one that continues to generate income while it is on YouTube, and Google pays me. When I write a book, there are royalties. When I buy a house and rent it, the rent is passive income. That is enough illustration. Starting now, I suggest cultivating a vocation so that you don't depend on a salary. A salary is temporary; today it is here but tomorrow it may not be. When someone tells me that their salary is 100,000 dollars a month and that, hence, their finances are just fine, I say: And do you have any income other than those 100,000 dollars that will continue to come in even if you stop working? It is common to see the surprised look on their faces. I'm not impressed by a high salary since continuing to receive it doesn't always depend on you. It also depends on the will of the person who hired you and of market swings. As high as it might be and irrespective of whether you are a prestigious executive or a manager or a corporate employee, a salary is what you receive for your work, for following a schedule, meeting goals, being away from your family, having a thousand meetings a week, and/or "living on a plane," but the main benefits won't be for you but rather for the one who pays you. From my point of view, financial progress doesn't come from your high salary but rather from the passive income you generate. Forget the salary, forget payday if you want to progress financially. And remember: it's not a coincidence that 'employed' is a synonym of 'used' in the dictionary or that we often see this in practice.

You might think you were born to be an employee. But from my experience, I can tell you that life pushes you to take action, and then you won't want to go back.

There are people who dedicate themselves to working in areas where demand is declining, and thus it turns out to be worthwhile to ask: will what I am doing have an increasing number of purchasers or more people who are interested in it? Will it require more people? Or will there be less demand that will make me obsolete like the old vinyl records or photographic film? Is it very smart to work hard for many years just to aspire to a lower salary in the future than what they are currently paying you due to your status as an employee? To me this isn't very smart. I repeat, it is smarter to use what you are paid in wages to build assets that generate income that, in the future, will turn your pension into a plus, a complement rather than that mirage into which you put all your expectations for a quality of life. How sad to hear people say, starting when they are very young, "when I retire with a pension," and go on to enumerate a list of dreams. However, we are still in the culture of the pension. A person with a financial education shouldn't worry about their pension. They should be concerned about building assets that generate an income. The majority of people won't to be able to retire with a pension, and if they do, they will do so with an income that is clearly inferior to what they enjoyed during their working years.

This doesn't mean that I think you should quit your job if you have one and enjoy it, but rather that you clearly understand that you shouldn't remain there indefinitely waiting for a pension. The idea of giving up security produces fear for the majority of people. Just thinking of it causes them anguish, but the price of security is that you never become rich. For someone who has no financial education, uncertainty about the future ends up devouring their dreams and goals. The day to day reality of payments and debts pushes their "reason why" onto the back burner. But their determination should be so strong and their motivation, a Level 10 motivation, so solid that there should be no fear whatsoever that could stop them, not even the fear of "throwing the cow over the cliff" in quiting their job. In the previous chapter, we saw how a fear can be crushed due to a motivation that is so strong that it pushes us to do and achieve what we previously thought was a dream, an illusion, madness. The true risk in not quiting is to remain, tethered to a job that you don't enjoy, and through which you won't be able to develop your greatest strengths.

Financial freedom is not achieved by having a good salary, but rather by living the life you want without relying on a salary.

I remember a couple that attended a breakfast we organized for some conference attendees and whose testimony demonstrated their fear of risking financial security.

They were professionals, a man and woman who were approximately 45 years old and had two children. They told us that, at one time, both of them were employed by important companies where they held positions for which each of them received high salaries. This economic security encouraged them to take on debt, which is not unlike of many people. They bought an apartment for themselves and their children and a car that they paid for in monthly installments. In addition, included among their fixed expenses was the education of their children at high-ranking schools with expensive enrollment fees, the daily maintenance of their home, and once in a while a vacation at some beach within the country in order to take a break from the exhausting routine in the city.

Everything seemed in order until rumors of a reorganization of the company where the husband worked began to go around and, ultimately, became a reality and he was laid off. Of course, this included a compensation which made it possible for him to "stay afloat until something new came along." Time went by and the situation remained stable but money was running out and his wife's income was not enough, even though it covered the debts, to support items such as education which was the most valuable thing for the family at this time. It was necessary to take on new debt with banks.

Moreover, in spite of having gone to job interviews, the man still hadn't found a new job and was on the waiting list at some companies. The reality was that, because of his age, he was no longer the "ideal" candidate they were looking for. Little by little the anguish in the home grew increasingly worse and reached the limit when she was also told that she wouldn't be working at the company she was employed at any more. The situation had become critical and began to turn desperate.

Hell is not a place; it's doing something you hate while others become rich doing something they love.

The alternative that they came to was to create their own business. A courageous decision, the fruit of extreme situations in their lives. They needed to reach the point where they were "against the ropes" and "the water was up to their necks" in order to realize that their salaries were temporary and that they might stop receiving it at any moment.

Indeed, when they made the decision, they were very bold since they went into a business in which they had no previous experience: real estate.

Leveraging a web page that they created, using networks of contacts, and taking advantage of technology, they have succeeded in picking up their way of life again and reaching a level of income through their determination that is even higher than what they had previously earned between the two of them. Their salaries had apparently opened up possibilities for them and certainly that is the way it was at the beginning, but later on, it put limits on them although they didn't even realize it. These limits were the boundaries of a zone we have spoken of, the comfort zone, within which they believed that everything would be guaranteed.

Throughout my experience I have been able to determine some "recipes" for building the passive income we are talking about and leveraging the social networks and YouTube to increase it. The first recipe has to do with a primary activity that generates cash flow for you. Let me explain: just as we say that it is very important for an oil company to find more petroleum, for a bank to lend more money, or for a cement plant to produce more cement and sell it, it is vital that a person's main activity—the one he dedicates his time to, the one that is his strength—produce enough monthly income to enable him to constantly save or make investments.

It is frequently said that you should save between 10 and 20% of your salary or fixed income. In general, those who listen to this advice put off their savings for the end of the month to see if anything should happen to be left over. If you are in a situation now in which you have a fixed salary, I suggest that you set aside your savings as soon as you receive your paycheck at the beginning of the month and not at the end when there may not be anything left. Of course, what is most desirable is for that money to produce some profit for you from the moment you put it into savings. I repeat, don't wait to save until the end of the month when you see what you have left, that is, if there is anything left. Invest a part of every monthly paycheck in assets that generate an income. Pretend that these funds that you invested don't exist anymore and based on what is left plan your expenditures.

What could happen? You realize that the proportion that you didn't save and are going to use for regular expenses isn't enough and won't cover everything. That's great! You will begin to feel the urgency of generating other sources of income. Excellent news for a purple cow which grows under pressure and is willing to start searching for more passive income that will pay for the expenses he has incurred. And what is even better: the money you saved or invested at the beginning will be making your capital grow. It should be noted that the passive income pays the monthly expenses that ensure the quality of life I want, not the ones I need to survive; remember this principle very well. And don't forget that the lack of savings also occurs because you didn't go into alternatives other than the traditional ones whether because of fears that paralyze you, lack of knowledge or because you are still wasting your time when you work on something other than your "reason why."

A second recipe for generating passive income has to do precisely with the analysis you do when you recognize that your fixed income isn't enough. Let's suppose that there is money that, like a salary, comes in regularly. After putting money into your fixed savings or investment, the next question you should ask yourself is: how much money comes in per month without our having to produce it directly or, in other words, do we receive funds monthly apart from our salary? Do we receive money from dividends, bonuses, interest, rent, commissions or royalties?

Do we have an apartment or a property that produces an income for us? Do we receive money because we are investing partners in a restaurant and profits are periodically shared with us? Or do we definitely not receive anything like that? If you don't have a passive income or any income other than your salary, then, the day you get sick or suffer from some type of disability that does not allow you to continue working, you won't have any more income. The flow of money will stop abruptly and you won't have alternatives. Begin to sow and cultivate sources of passive income. You will think: "I don't have enough money. I can barely get what I need monthly to make ends meet. I can't set aside anything for other investments." Under those circumstances, I have to reaffirm that if you have a Level 10 motivation, a solid and transcendental "reason why," this shouldn't be a limitation. Perhaps at the moment you don't have the money to begin to buy assets, bonds or stocks, or property. It doesn't matter. There is an old proverb that says, "Constant dropping wears away a stone". So don't underestimate capital, however small it is, because with a clear purpose, it will increase the asset holdings that will make it possible for you to generate passive income. You will begin to see money work for you and replace you because you may not always want to work at the same pace that you do today. Don't worry about the lack of money. Focus on having ideas that will produce it. If you have capital without ideas, the capital will vanish; have ideas without capital, and the capital will come. I can testify to this. Invertir Mejor was born with the resources to put an idea into practice: a seminar on investment over the Internet when the majority didn't even have a computer in the house and Internet was barely taking off in the region. It was a success. And from then on, the funds that gave rise to my company began to emerge in an era in which I was earning less than a thousand dollars a month. Being aware of the low income in Latin America, I have uploaded a series of videos to our YouTube channel on how to get business ideas, how to make progress if you have a low wage, how to invest without enough money, how to forget about your salary, and many videos on passive income that you are invited to enjoy and to put into practice.

Ideas are the new name for money in the 21st century.

The third recipe is to be connected to making a more efficient use of expenses. There are good debts and there are bad debts; there are good expenses and bad expenses. One should not reduce all expenses they have in a month. There are people who specialize in reducing expenditures, but are very limited in producing income. Expenses must generate income. For example, spending on technology and education shouldn't be reduced. If I reduce access to technology and knowledge, my income will be reduced; therefore, that wasn't an expense that was reduced, rather a cost that was incurred. Any financial coach will tell you: increase income, lower expenses or, in other words, survive. I don't share that idea. There are times when spending more enables us to discover new revenue. I'm not talking about irresponsible spending nor of paying 36 installments on your credit card because "that way you don't feel it." Nothing like that. I am talking about sending myself messages of abundance. I am talking about telling the future, "I will pay for what I'm spending today on what I like, on what I want with my income. I have no doubt of that. And since I liked what I bought, I will generate more income that will continue to pay for it." I have to think of new business ideas that will pay for it. We are going to explain this with an example.

Why is it more cost-effective to travel in first class than in economy class? What message am I sending myself when I travel in first class? First of all, since it will certainly be more pleasant than traveling in economy class and you will possibly end up liking the comfort you enjoyed, the message would be: "This is what I deserve, what my family and the people I love deserve." Therefore, if I want to retain this level of comfort and, by making an effort, I was able to pay for it once, I need to work out business ideas to continue paying for it. That's the mindset of the rich person. In contrast, if I don't take on the risk of going after what I deserve and remain in my comfort zone where it is unnecessary to generate new ideas for new and higher income, I will remain poor. Secondly, if I pay a higher price to travel in executive class, I am showing confidence that the future will be even better than the present and that, as a result, I will have the income I need to meet the cost of today's expenses. Something different occurs when I travel in row 30 of the airplane next to the bathroom imprisoned by the person ahead of me who, when he tilts his seat back, traps me as if I were in a can of tuna. And why travel that way? Well, because the future may be gray or not very encouraging, so it would be better to not incur expenses. Does this ring a bell, my dear reader? Imprisoned as if in a sardine can, with a bunch of people around me who have everything they need to travel in first class—health, abilities, immediate pressing needs, children to raise—but too full of fear to live the life they deserve supposedly because the future is uncertain, supposedly because with what they pay in economy class, they can cover tuition, and supposedly because, in the end, we are all traveling on the same plane. That is a lie. That is the way that the poor man's mindset traps the majority. The mindset of the rich person chooses both things, not just one. High schools or first class? Both!

Remember: if, on some occasions, your expenses rise and push you against the ropes, the pressing needs will make that genius that we all have inside blossom. There are people who think they lack nothing, but who don't have anything to spare either, and they believe everything is fine that way. They think that is life. They are, in my opinion, people who conform and are letting the opportunity to get more resources, earn more money, and enjoy a better quality of life go by.

What, then, is the invitation? It is *not to worship irresponsible spending*. Here, I am talking about an expense that forms me, that demands of me, that forces me to create assets, to seek business deals that will pay for those expenses. These are expenses that make me happy, that increase my chances of making rapid progress, that give me greater alternatives to choose from, and that fill me with useful information and experiences. They are expenses that make me feel like I am living and not just surviving. If you are in a comfort zone, perhaps you need to spend more than you have coming in in a month and thus be overdrawn so that your creative genius is stimulated.

The fourth recipe for increasing passive income is to make technology take on a leading role. The first thing that I would recommend is that if you have already discovered what your talent is and where the demand is among the public for what you offer, if you have already decided to start your own business, have you thought of setting up an *online* store, for example? Have you analyzed how to take advantage yet of digital media and social networks to multiply your efforts? Remember that you want to increase your income exponentially. You want to make quantum leaps rather than go "step by step." You want to travel in first class from now on. To attain that, you should generate income with the business you have, but think about the fact that the amount of business and sales will multiply if you and your business are "cloned" thanks to technology. There won't be one source of income anymore but rather several working twenty-four hours a day that need a minimal investment compared to the results that can be obtained. If you haven't gotten many of the things that you want in life, you have to make yourself do things that you haven't done before since if you keep doing the same, you cannot expect different results. At what point will you realize that your finances are progressing? When your passive income pays for the quality of life that you want to have. Or if you want to see it another way, when you can cover your fixed expenses for several months without working just by leveraging your passive income. That is when you will be able to say that you have progressed financially.

It is clear at this point that only by generating passive income will you achieve financial progress and that the path you need to follow to create it is the use of technology, Internet, and social networks. Have a channel on YouTube that provides useful content (on www.invertirmejor.com and www.ganardineroconvideos.com we tell you how to do it). Put videos up on a regular basis with suggestive names and a high emotional component. Creating accounts on the main social networks, dealing with people's needs, interacting with your followers, and being constant in sending messages are essential practices. If you have your own website, so much the better. This is a seal of distinction and identity. It is your own brand. "Why a website, Juan Diego, if I don't have a product to promote?," you might be wondering. Remember: you are a product.

Traveling first class doesn't make you better than others. It just sends yourself a message of abundance.

An excuse to not to do these things is to say (and convince yourself) that you don't have the time or money to do so. Nothing but excuses. We talk about investments that are made without money and I even put videos focused on that topic up on our YouTube channel. When the excuse arrives, poverty appears. And another major pretext I run into very frequently is the fear produced by social networks and even the possibility of using the computer and the Internet for something other than playing, betting, venting one's feelings, or checking e-mail. If social networks and YouTube are the most powerful tools of our time, we have to leverage them in order to generate passive income. If you set up your own business but this means that you are spending a lot of time behind a counter, it isn't profitable, whereas if you have it on social networks where millions of people are watching what you do, that is different. What is more, many commercial premises where products of various kinds were advertised and sold have already migrated to social networks. They are exhibited and sold there at no cost.

I always say ignorance underestimates what it cannot explain, and this is what happens when we speak of technology applied in business and in the construction of wealth to reach financial freedom. Nowadays, it has nothing to do with how hard you work but how hard money and technology work for you. Computers and telephones have to be assets that generate income, and social networks should be the main channels by means of which we find those who are willing to buy the goods or services that we are offering. In addition, to the extent that more people get a mobile device, there will also be more people who use the social networks, and this trend is irreversible.

It is no secret, therefore, that the social networks are producing countless businesses and relationships, the spread of information is increasing, and habits are changing. At the time I wrote this book, five out of ten young people between the ages of 25 and 34 were using social networks at work; 5 out of every 10 people are using the networks while watching television; 1 out of every 3 young people between the ages of 18 and 24 were using social networks while they were in the bathroom. This isn't simply something to be surprised about; it is a great opportunity to take advantage of the market and of new consumption patterns that guide business relationships today on a worldwide level. Traditional industries have had to connect themselves to this change, and those who don't, succumb rapidly. One example was the toy industry which had to innovate when they were displaced by the huge supply of video games and applications that consumers found. They could have hundreds of games available on one device and no longer depended on a board that offered only one game. Not to mention the music, movies, or information industries, which have had to reinvent themselves and mutate to a digital form, fighting hard against free offers and pirating.

If we look at the securities and investment market, this has changed. Before, only a few people could participate in it, and they were intermediaries. The image of the traditional investor in the middle of a frenzied excitement of buying and selling on the floor of the stock market is a picture from films of Wall Street. Today and thanks to our interconnectivity and Internet, the markets have become more open, changed, and the opportunities that emerge from them have become massive. From your own house, as I have demonstrated countless times in my face-to-face and online investment seminars over the Internet for non-experts, you can buy stocks, foreign currencies, or commodities through accounts that you can open with just a little money on platforms that work in Spanish, have good technical support, and offer the option of practicing first on test accounts.

I listen to people who say they don't want to use social networks because, according to them, they see nothing useful on them, just things that discourage them such as smears, insults, or gossip that they aren't interested in. There is a lot of that—that is partially true—but at the same time, the number of people and companies that are there is immense and should serve as a basis for providing messages that legitimately distance themselves from the large amount of superfluous information present.

Social networks are a powerful source for business and contacts. Don't use them just to vent yourself and share your opinions. Make sure you understand them.

The majority only use social networking sites to vent themselves. Vent yourself if you want to, but also search for benefits. Help someone, generate more relationships and business opportunities. You have to look for an additional effect and one that will add value to your "reason why." Someone retweeted what you published because it was intelligent or useful. This increased the number of your followers and it became a trending topic. All of this can happen if you use your head to manage your networks. When you begin to see them differently (as we have done with Invertir Mejor, where we've reached the point where they are our main source of income) and not just as sites where you and everyone else vent their feelings, this powerful tool will make sense to you. Whoever lacks the determination to make progress will always find excuses not to do it, and the same thing happens with technology.

Anyone who doesn't have the will or readiness to learn to use it for their financial growth and leverage it to the maximum once they can manage it has a poverty mindset and will never make the quantum leaps that the digital era allows. "I don't know how to upload a video, I don't know how to use a camera, I'm not good at talking in public, I don't know what to say with so few characters, Facebook is for uploading pictures of my friends,"—I hear a myriad of pretexts when it comes to social networks. These pretexts block and hold back the mindset we should maintain and cultivate day to day, second to second, in order to prosper. Remember: I either complain or adapt; I either adjust or become extinguished.

We have helped hundreds of people to create their online businesses and to optimize their use of the social networks and YouTube. This means a lot since you can make good use of time by using forms of business that operate 24-hours a day with minimal intervention from their creator and multiplying the effects and benefits for many people at the same time. One video of yours on YouTube, for example, is nothing but a clone that works for you 365 days of the year without rest or asking for a raise. We ourselves had to go through this learning curve when we created Invertir Mejor in 2004 and discovered later that YouTube was the most suitable tool for exponentially multiplying the number of people who consulted us about how to achieve financial liberty, how to invest over the Internet and, later, how to find their "reason why" or purpose in life. We made videos to help them and we made sure that, in addition to useful content, there was also publicity about the company in these videos. Eureka! Many people saw the videos and ended up buying the products in the www.invertirmejor.com virtual store that were combos, online seminars or programs for traders. Those results, of course, didn't happen from one day to the next. But perseverance and nonconformity are purple virtues. We went from 100 views of our videos per day in 2009 to more than 70,000 views per day in 2016. We are continuing to grow steadily to date, and you can see us any time, from anywhere in the world, and participate in our online seminars which, of course, you can do at any time without any need for my physical presence or that of my team of advisers. What is more, some of the Invertir Mejor products already have the goal of helping people get passive income and, literally, live at the expense of the social networks and YouTube.

What is powerful about business and investments online is that they continue flowing while you do other things and continue to produce income. When you refine your products, when you really know what people need, profitability starts increasing, and you can dedicate more time to your family, for example. Stop being a white cow like those who say, "I am going to work more to see if I earn more" and become a purple cow that says, "I can earn more working less." Keep in mind the fact that "working less" is not synonymous with spending your time asleep at home; it means that technology and money are working harder than you are.

Last century you did 20 projects and they paid you 20 times. In this new century you work once and get paid over and over. This is another name for: passive income.

This experience has allowed us to identify some guide-lines that will be useful when you start your own exploration of the social networks in search of better income. The first thing is that if you have already found what your business opportunity is and what it is you are going to offer, you have to specialize. Ask yourself what you really are interested in and what your talent relates to best. Remember that all of us, absolutely everyone, are products, so we are always sell-ing ourselves.

Secondly, search on the Internet to find out what there is that is close to what you offer. Study references that could be useful in creating your own distinctive way of doing what they do but doing it much better. Get inspiration from good practices and those things that work. That will be useful to you. Watch those who follow them, their role models, and follow them.

Third, if you are going to create various profiles on dif-ferent networks, make them consistent with each other. Connect them and have them duplicate each other. If you publish something on Twitter, there are ways to repeat this on Facebook or on Instagram or viceversa immediately. Today everything is interconnected. Get advice from people who are experts on the topic and from the material available to create a personal brand that unites your networks.

Fourth, and this should be your principle, give value to what you communicate. If you used to criticize social networks as places where people vented their feelings or published superfluous things, now that you use them, this is your opportunity to contribute with valuable informa-tion. Don't sell just for selling. Sell to improve the life of the thousands or millions of people who may read it. If you are going to duplicate information or share it, think of something useful with added value so that the content will act as a hook and people will listen to the news you give them. This can be summed up in one word: relevance. It should be relevant to others.

This has to do with something that has happened to us. There are people who contact us and send us their concerns on an individual basis. When we see that the answer could help other people, we publish the solution for everyone. Thus we spread knowledge and optimize the use of the networks as we reach more people, and we certainly save time and effort for others. If your videos help people, the Universe will reward that handsomely.

Fifth, the way you do it is also very important here. Providing content, helping people, satisfying needs by means of agile videos with notable visual quality, with a high emotional component, compelling, and that capture our attention with highly suggestive titles is the main objective. And it isn't a matter of money, it is a matter of resourcefulness, talent, ingenuity. There are people who say to me: "I don't have any money", and I tell them: "It isn't that you lack money, you lack ideas."

Of course, you have to learn how to use the platforms. This takes some time, but they are designed so that virtually anyone can do it. YouTube, for example, is believed to be perhaps the most powerful in the world and provides tutorials so you can take advantage of all their resources to the maximum. We have developed a website dedicated to supporting the creation of people's own channels for our partners and for the whole world called www.ganardineroconvideos.com. In it, we give some very specific guidelines for taking advantage of the earnings derived from advertising on YouTube, how to generate credibility, create confidence on the part of the audience and benefit from it as well as some technical tips to making better videos that are short and don't take long to make. The value of a video is that it facilitates the understanding of the one who watches it and requires less effort on the part of the one who makes it. Many people tell me: "Juan Diego, but I need a lot of views in order for Google to pay me for having my videos on YouTube." It is not about earning money just with people watching your videos. It is about people buying your products in the virtual store on your web site after seeing your videos because you captivated them.

The value of an entrepreneur, of a purple person who has decided that he is going to become rich, is that if he wants to generate new income, he will dare to do things that he wouldn't have done before, and leverage technology to do them. That's where the secret lies.

5

TIME FOR PLAN B

—

What motivated me to invest through the Internet and what did I find? In 2000, when I began to invest over the Internet, it was a groundbreaking thing in Latin America. That year I was moved by an intense desire: to stop investing in the same old thing. Investments aren't bad only when they pay a poor rate, but also when you don't learn anything from them. You can be sure that there is a double loss when you have your funds in a savings account, not simply because of the low interest they pay but also because you don't learn anything while the money is there. I like challenges. The uncertainty that the process of investing over the Internet involves is captivating. I enjoyed the risk that this type of investment involved. No one becomes rich without taking risks. So this challenge, this uncertainty, this not knowing what I would find by investing on the Internet motivated me a lot.

Second, someone once asked me: "Juan Diego, what guarantee do you have that you will get money through Internet-based investment?" I repeat, it was the year 2000. My answer was sincere: "No guarantee." The best investments don't guarantee their rate. Why do they guarantee you a 2% or 3% rate per year on a fixed income security? Because something that bad is easy to guarantee. The same thing is true of savings accounts and many other investments.

I was eager for knowledge and full of vigor. I wasn't seeking assurances that one investment or another would yield good fruit. Furthermore, I never forgot our grandparents' saying that has to encourage investors: "pioneers always have the best land." A pioneer, someone who risks himself to the unknown, is putting himself to the test, building himself up daily without fear; he cannot come in last of all because he will get the worst of the distribution. I wasn't afraid. Any inkling of fear was totally eclipsed by a Level 10 motivation which was to invest over the Internet.

What were those first markets in which I started to invest? Voluntary pension markets in Colombia and international stocks. Later, I began making the transition to the foreign currency market commonly known as Forex, and then I traded commodities such as oil, silver and gold, and finally, Colombian stocks and binary options, a new subject for me at the time, and one I will talk about later.

When I opened my first account to do business over the Internet with a broker called ETrade in the United States, I didn't even have an account abroad from which to wire the money. I had to enlist a person who would serve as a bridge. I paid him in pesos in Colombia and from his account he would send the funds to make the transactions on that platform, which was allowed at that time. I wasn't even making USD 1,000 as a university professor when I made this first investment. Someone might wonder if this lack of money was a problem for me at that time. No. I never see lack of money as a problem. I always see lack of money as an incentive to obtain it.

With some brokers, the minimum amount required to open an account and make transactions was exactly USD 1,000. That was almost my monthly salary at that time, but that didn't mean that I was going to regret my decision or that I would wait. Any worry or feeling of being alone due to the fact that none of my friends transacted business over the Internet was mitigated by the pleasure of making my own investments from a computer which seemed more like an abacus than anything else. Was I afraid at that time? Yes, of course, a lot, but it wasn't as strong as my motivation.

Instead of sticking a needle into their arms or swallowing some pills, many would be better off trying other drugs: binary options + forex + stocks.

I remember that during that period, my finger would be frozen above the computer keyboard on some occasions before clicking to buy or sell. My fears and the demons visited me trying to remind me that there was capital in play, not much, but in the end it was capital that could be lost when I invested it. "Who's afraid!", my inner self said to me. What do I recommend? Invite those fears to sit down at the table with you, invite your defects also. When they find themselves faced with a Level 10 motivation, they will bow their heads and disappear completely. The motivation was very clear: I wanted to become a role model on the subject of investment over the Internet. If you have level 6, 7, or 8 motivations, you will be part of the white cow universe that fills the planet and you will see how your defects and fears block your dreams and hinder your achievements. That doesn't happen with a Level 10 motivation.

One believes when he begins to invest over the Internet that more business means better business. I confess: I saw investments signs on that computer all day and today, I have reached the conclusion that I had imagined many of them. My desire to transact business and my desire to experience how it felt to click on a purchase or selling order were so strong that I saw signs that didn't exist. This feverish spirit, this craving, led me to do things that were as implausible as the following: when I migrated to the Forex market, I made a trade at 9:00 p.m., for example. Let's assume that I bought a euro/dollar pair and turned off the computer. I went to bed late and before falling asleep, doubts began to attack me. "Why did you buy a euro/dollar pair if Europe is in recession and Germany has tons of problems?" I tried to control myself unsuccessfully and finally got up, turned on the computer and closed the transaction. In other words, I sold what I had bought, which allowed me to sleep peacefully that night without the anxiety of having a transaction I was in doubt about.

The next day before breakfast, I turned on the computer again and what you are probably imagining right now had happened. The euro had risen in price and I would have profited had I not closed the operation. At that instant, I could not stand myself. Fortunately, I did not do that again. Why? Because if there is anything that polishes the individual, if there is anything that polishes the human being, it is investing on the Internet. It is not only a course in geography that invites you to learn about many countries around the world, their currencies, their products, their governments, news, and economies, but also the virtues and defects you have as a human being are exposed when you invest over the Internet.

Why would you change a way of acting which is already farfetched? Because you're changing your personality as a trader. What does this mean in plain language? You are gathering experience, polishing yourself more, controlling yourself more, becoming more patient, but above all, what helps the most is that you start seeing that fewer trades often mean better profits.

There are those who are afraid of some investments, but they have their money in a savings account. Without earning or learning. That really makes me afraid.

At one point I did day trading or high frequency trades, which many people are engaged in today. I respect and understand it. It has a special adrenaline: it's fascinating to watch as capital comes an goes when you're buying at 8:00 am and selling five minutes later, reentering the market at 9:00 am and trading throughout the day as time passes by in a flash. It interested me until I stumbled across a magical book called *The Intelligent Investor*, a book that I still find greatly useful, which was published for the first time in 1949 by the late Benjamin Graham, father of financial analysis— and mentor of Warren Buffet, by the way.

Graham said something which over time has impressed me deeply: "the more you trade, the less you keep." A much more restful, judicious, methodical, less nervous trading form, which can be cultivated over the years can give you a greater profitability than when you are making transactions throughout the whole day. What is more, by moving away from transactions like the one mentioned above in which I got up and closed it to be at peace, you are now sending a message to yourself that says: "Don't get excited when you win, or when you lose." The good trader is like the good poker player; he maintains the same level of excitement during all stages of the game.

By the years 2007 and 2008, we had a very interesting team of traders at Invertir Mejor with whom we demonstrated a methodology that was a resounding success. It was a methodology of trading based on news, a real addiction, which I explained in my investment seminars on the Internet.

At that time, the trades were so large and profits often came so fast that if we literally hadn't had our feet on the ground, we would have gone crazy. Indeed, as I made public when it happened, a broker called ACM Markets banned me in 2008 due to the fact that, according to them, we earned money very fast. In other words, we did totally leveraged trades in which we closed the operations within a period of 1 to 5 minutes with all of the adrenaline in the world and had good results. We were committed and we sent that message, to feel nothing, to the body.

What do you mean, Juan Diego, are you saying you can send that message to yourself? Of course, you can do that. Perhaps you have invested and made a profit. You don't believe it. Pretend that it didn't happen and everything remains the same. The good investor doesn't believe he is the greatest one in the world when he makes a profit nor the worst when he loses. Those who have attended my Invertir Mejor seminar on investments over the Internet have proven this.

The message I sent myself was: "You can't let yourself feel anything, otherwise you will go mad." When you have good, fast and very fruitful profits, you will feel like you were born for that and that you will have only profits. But if there were a loss, the message would probably be different, a diametrically different and frustrating one. So I chose to not feel anything at all as a mental tactic: neither one nor the other, to neither sleep on my laurels of triumph nor be frightened by the defeats or losses.

Look at how the old paradigm that "the beginning of an endeavor tells you what the end will be like" is disproved. In the first ten trades I made in 2004 when investing in the foreign exchange market over the Internet, my results, as many of you know, were as follows: I lost on each one. A chimpanzee taught to throw a coin in the air in order to decide whether to buy or sell would have had more success than me at that moment.

But my Level 10 motivation was in charge. I wasn't afraid, or as a friend of mine said, "what does one more blade spin matter to a fan."

I persevered and five years later we had the best signal provider in the world on Forex, and the profits we produced resulted not only in our being banned by the broker but also my receiving a call from the regional manager of Bancolombia, the largest bank in Colombia, in which she said something like this to me: "Juan Diego, I need to meet you because there is something that confuses me. There are people who are doubling the amount in their accounts within six months and they say they are following in your footsteps."

Her concern was to understand how her clients who, for instance, had USD 5,000 in their accounts one day could be withdrawing USD 15,000 six months later, money from licit transactions. It is very simple, I told her: every broker, whoever they are, allows a statement of the account with the history of the movements made to be downloaded so that when the person brings the funds into the country, he can demonstrate the source of the money to any entity. This was completely new for everyone so it raised a lot of suspicions and, ultimately, that is the price that pioneers pay.

"The last shall be first." This only looks nice in the Bible. I prefer: "Pioneers always have the best land."

What is the moral of this? When investing over the Internet, there is no virtue that is more important than perseverance and patience. Don't believe the paradigms, "don't believe everything you hear" that the white cows want us to believe. You weren't born for that; that the beginning of an endeavor tells you what the end will be like. None of that. Just live off get strength from skeptics because they will leverage your progress. Be glad that even at home they are saying: "are you still wasting time on that computer?" Just stick to it and continue. It is an exercise in control. For a purple cow, this is paradise. You will celebrate with them, you will invite them to your table to eat caviar with the best wines and, without holding any resentment, it will be a pleasure to see how those who didn't believe in your dreams, who don't know what it means to persevere and follow your intuition, congratulate you and enjoy the honey of your triumph.

There is no virtue more important than patience and perseverance when it comes to doing business, no other. I have known successful traders who are architects, lawyers, veterinarians, people with limited financial formation but who are determined, patient, and hungry and have achieved amazing results. The key is in never losing that hunger or ambition. The day you realize that you have experienced an unexpected attack of conformity, the day you realize that the comfort zone is part of your life, react! Because I don't want any more white cows, I don't want more people who accommodate themselves. I want people who are determined and hungry with that hunger which will lead them to success.

What suggestions might I give today? The first is that your income shouldn't depend on trading even if you are a successful trader or even if you are good at investing over the Internet or doing business on the Internet. I experienced several years of trading, particularly between 2005 and 2009. It was my main source of income especially leveraging on the Forex market because the stock market didn't allow as much leverage as the foreign exchange market did.

Nevertheless, and in spite of the excellent results that can be obtained, I don't recommend that this be your only source of income. There has to be an additional reason for generating income, and this is basically what I look into thoroughly with my Purple, Gold or Elite partners in Invertir Mejor when I help them analyze in depth what they came into this world for. If trading is your life purpose, go ahead. But if it's not, do not depend on it for your income.

In 2000 I was asked: "What guarantee do you have that investing over the Internet will go well for you?" None: the best investments don't guarantee their rate.

You have a talent that you are probably not using the way you should. When you look at your finances and see that they are limited, I can assure you that this is because you haven't developed the talent you came into the world with nor have you shown it to the thousands of people who might be interested in it. I am convinced of that. When you find the answer to the question of why you came into this world and dedicate yourself to it, that is, dive into it, you will never have problems concerning investment.

What happens in practice? The majority of people die without knowing what they were good at. They vegetate at a job and adapt to it. They even begin to behave in ways they previously deplored. How? By only smiling on the 15th and 30th of every month, when they get their paycheck. They hate Mondays, concentrate on how much their salary will increase next year, talk about things like their pension, worry about the regular bonus and other regrettable behavior. I'm not against employees. I was one of them. I am only against working on something that you don't enjoy and that isn't what you came into this world to do, something that doesn't resonate with you. There is no guaranteed reincarnation. Thus, it is crucial that you find the "reason why" you came into this world not only for personal satisfaction, but also as a purpose that would enable you to obtain more income and not depend on trading.

There are people who say, "Juan Diego, this month was very bad because I bought many euros and the price dropped." That is a contingency, something transitory. It cannot be your reason for living nor what determines whether the month was good or bad. All months are good if you invested in your life purpose every day. It shouldn't matter if a stock or currency rises in price because you are equipped, financially educated, and developing your "reason why."

There are other people who say: "the economy is doing very well, so I am fine; or the economy is very bad, so naturally things aren't going well for me." This is false. A person with financial education and a clear "reason why" makes progress in both economically difficult periods and in great ones. It doesn't depend on the trading. The difficulties the economy imposes on it will help them to leverage themselves.

You might be saying: "Juan Diego, this idea about investments over the Internet is very interesting, but I have two problems: I have neither the time nor the knowledge to make investments on my own." Additionally, you may not even have a computer or a good Internet connection. But all of this can change.

In 2000, as far as I knew, there were no signal providers, that is, people or systems that, using technology, would trade for you so that purchase or sales orders would enter your dummy or real account. There was no one who could do business for you. There was no possibility of putting them to the test in a dummy account, and then later, based on the results, use them in a real account. Today there are thousands of signal providers that can make up for your shortcomings. I repeat, there are expert systems or people that can transact business for you in dummy accounts and subsequently in real accounts, especially on Forex platforms. This is an option that I suggest using today after you check each provider's record. Indeed, the best of the scenarios is the one in which this alternative is used for the provider to trade your funds while at the same time you have an account you manage yourself to see how much progress you are making. So, can I have an account I manage myself and another one that is managed by a signal provider, someone who transacts business or trades for me? Of course, and that is a good scenario for you to get to know each other. There are people who are afraid to make transactions on "demo" accounts, but that is where they find out what they are made of.

When are you really going to begin to be concerned about money? When you have that money invested in a market. What do you think about the Chinese yuan, New Zealand's trade deficit, the employment problem in Canada? Nothing, unless you have invested in markets that are related to those areas. Have investments in China and New Zealand, do business with the Canadian dollar and you'll see if this news matters to you or not. Whether just to make demands of yourself, get involved in the markets, or broaden your reality, you need to invest over the Internet. A person's financial reality is based on what that person believes is financially possible. "Nothing will change until the person's reality changes, and this will only be possible when that person is able to go beyond the fears and doubts that he has placed on himself." Fear does not give you money, fear paralyzes.

The greatest risk is living a mediocre life, below your possibilities, and one in which fear, rather than your dreams, plays the leading role.

Another suggestion, besides not depending on trading and resorting to signal providers: by investing over the Internet there is a greater possibility of earning money if you correctly make use of a method called *leverage*. Leveraging has other definitions, but here it means investing with other people's money—and, if you use good investment methods, it allows you to see your earnings rise as if in an elevator while those of others walk up the stairs.

If you have a good investment methodology, please let yourself be tempted by leveraging. With a good hand, the good player increases his bet, some would say. Throughout our lives complain that we don't have money, but the world is full of money. Even leveraging your capital 300 or 400 times on some trading platforms is frightening, and we don't use that since we lack the guts to do so. So, the problem is not the capital since the money is there, provided to the brokers themselves by the financial system. What you have to find for yourself or through third parties is a good investment methodology that will allow you to make better use of that leveraging in order to transact much larger trades.

More suggestions: there is a recent topic that has gathered a lot of interest and is related to binary options. I don't know how long this market will operate, but whether or not it continues, keep in mind what I say here.

The first thing I can say is that you have to be careful, very careful who you open the account with. Always verify that the broker is a regulated one, that they are monitored and have been in the market for a significant time.

The second is that binary options are not to be used in the market at any time, but only when the trend for what you are going to buy or sell is very clear. Let's assume that Barcelona plays a football match against Levant. The expected result is that Barcelona will win given their history of games won, players, and playing styles. Everything indicates that the result will be in favor of the Catalan team.

Suppose someone says: "If the Barcelona team wins, I will give you 7 dollars, but if it loses, you pay me 10." It is very clear that the options of winning those 7 dollars are much higher.

The probabilities are greater than that. When the market is very clear, transact binary options, but begin with prudence and, first, practice as always. But if the game were between Barcelona and Real Madrid, where the probabilities may be fifty-fifty, and it is not obvious who'll win, don't choose binary options.

Last of all, remember that investments over the Internet aren't limited to foreign currency, stocks, and commodities. There is a person working for you for free 24 hours a day, 365 days a year to produce money, who is not asking how much you are going to raise his salary next year. This person is called "a video of yours on the Internet." Be obsessed with passive income. The Internet is not just for buying or selling financial assets.

Let me tell you there is no greater happiness, financially speaking, than receiving a check from Google for the videos you recorded once and that continue earning money for the rest of your life. What are we waiting for? "Juan Diego, my financial situation is precarious. Besides that, I'm scared of being in front of a camera. I don't express myself well nor do I look good." Don't make more excuses, instead, create a motivation. For example, "that the income from the Internet be what pays for my children's education." I can assure you that this way you will be motivated enough to take advantage of that tool to the max and learn to speak in front of a camera, express yourself, upload a video, and improve every day, but only if that motivation is strong enough.

Finally, the importance of attitude. On one occasion I said: "I will shuffle forward on my knees with a white cow on my shoulders, and in the middle of a long trail, I will stop so that she, not I, can drink a little water." That is the attitude that I have in order to be in the supercharged mode, to soar, and conquer the world. What is your attitude?

6

ATTITUDE

—

We have talked about the fact that in the face of adversity, crises, and scenarios of seeming uncertainty, we need to reconfigure the panorama in our favor and draw out the strength and vigor to focus on our "reason why." There are no better incentives for discovering what we are made of than those times when we think there is no way out, we are against the ropes, and in which it seems like there is no tomorrow.

In difficult times like those, we need to have our Level 10 motivations, the ones that will lead us on the road of abundance, at hand. Taking advantage of the difficult times, looking at them from a different point of view and even converting them into a trampoline of quantum leaps is what we have called "leveraging ourselves." It means that we use something that seems to be an obstacle, a fear, comments that try to bring us down, situations that seem to have no escape, and we convert them into a pillar that supports our determination to become rich.

We have also seen that it is the monetary emergencies, the extreme situations in which we apparently have no money, that shape us and demand more of us. This is the only way we will discover our talents for generating new revenue. To be more precise, passive income that makes it possible to pay for the quality of life we deserve.

When you are going through those difficult moments, they seem insurmountable, but in the end, you know that if it hadn't been for them, you wouldn't have been victorious. It is in the clay, the asphalt, the difficulty where you will be shaped as a human being and when you will show the world what you are made of. To put it vulgarly, "Shit nourishes and increases your defenses". While you eat it, it tastes terrible, but over time, you will discover that if you hadn't eaten it, you wouldn't have become a much stronger person. That being the case, as long as you have even a tiny trickle of a two-week salary, great things won't happen to you. And the thing is you won't need those great things, the body won't ask for them. You are in your comfort zone. In contrast, it is when you don't have anything that the most brilliant ideas occur to you, and you are forced to produce. It is when you are in the middle of adversity that you ask yourself: "What do I know how to do? What am I going to do to produce and get different results?"

Behind all this there is something key: the attitude. For me, your attitude is the only sustainable competitive advantage that exists. Think of this phrase, and the deep meaning it has: "The same water that hardens an egg softens a potato." Thus, it's not the circumstances that matter. What's important is the attitude with which you handle them and how that facilitates achieving things, not just material ones but spiritual ones too.

We have huge challenges in that attitude-wealth link. It's an act of irresponsibility to die poor and leave behind those who follow you, who depend on you in rivers of tears, blood, and debts and making them suffer when you have everything you need to be rich and could have given them better results during your life.

It is very common to hear people say that one problem calls another and when you have one difficulty, all of them come down on you together, and, therefore, how are they going to keep up an optimistic attitude towards life if life keeps them mired in a maelstrom of bad news. Many other people ask how they can make progress, how to have a good attitude when their life overwhelms them with one grief after another. I ask a different question: and will a bad attitude, low energy, or notable pessimism help you to get out of the difficult situation that you are in? I don't think so.

If we think about the origin of many fortunes and the wealth of people who are role models today, their capital emerged in the eras of difficulty, in the middle of a crisis. I have always said: A country in crisis (which is a bad term and one I don't like much, but let's accept it temporarily) is a paradise of opportunities. Why? Because when so many are crying, it is very profitable to sell handkerchiefs, and those of us who enjoy a good attitude came into the world for this, to sell handkerchiefs. There are many people who wonder why things happen to them and that makes them victims, but others like us ask the reason why something happens to us and that makes us entrepreneurs and opens doors and opportunities for us.

While you think that the world, the economy or your country are in crisis, many become millionaires at the expense of your pessimism.

I remember someone who was once talking to me and complaining about the lack of money and the conditions being imposed on his business by a crisis in the economy. I asked him then how many human beings he was helping by satisfying some need, how many he solved some problem for, how many he gave a chance to live a better life. He couldn't answer me at that point but if, in the midst of a crisis the answer is "few people," then his income will most certainly be low. If, however, during a time of crisis you succeed in benefiting many people through your work, you will succeed in gathering a lot of resources. Crisis is a ubiquitous word, and that's why I don't like it. While you are using that word, there are, at the same time, millions of people who are having a great life and even benefiting from what you have called a crisis.

People constantly complain and say: "No one will give me a chance." A purple cow, someone who is extraordinary, doesn't need someone to give him opportunities; he sees them, smells them, creates them, and takes advantage of them. Before we complain about how difficult things are, let's really look at what our *pro-wealth* attitude is. Let's ask how much we are capitalizing what we see, hear, read and, asking ourselves the "reason why" things happen to us or if, instead, we are hiding behind the "why" they happened which is synonymous with a person who complains.

At times, and this is something that is very rooted in our Latin American cultures, we tend to believe that the difficulties and crises appear in our lives because "it was God's will" and that we will get out of them "if God wants that to happen." And there are other phrases we use daily like these that reinforce that belief that things happen because of a divine will and are totally outside of our control.

What I think with respect to that is that what God wants of us above all is determination, God wants attitude, God wants you to progress and help many others to progress also with everything he has given you. He doesn't want so much lamentation, nor so much resignation. There is a phrase that I like a lot: "Pray as if everything depended on God but work as if everything depended on you." I think that the attitude there is also a determining factor. Don't blame God for everything, no, no, no. Where is your perseverance? Where is your attitude? Where is your determination and persistence? Remember: the Universe takes pictures. If you seem very determined to it, it will send you what you deserve, and give you more merit points. But if you are simply resigned and send messages of defeat all the time, what will the Universe send you? Nothing good.

It involves not leaving everything to drift and waiting to see what happens. As we said before: The person who takes over the reins of his life is free. Not the one who prays and expects things to change by themselves and by a miracle. You have to help yourself and change that lazy, complacent mindset of someone who just sits there and watches time go by.

For me, the question that can help me the most to not only develop a better attitude but also progress is: What motivation do I have in life? Motivations chemically help attitudes improve. Motivations eclipse defects. Motivations activate dreams. Motivations prevent suicides. Having a Level 10 motivation is synonymous with having reasons to hold on to a good attitude. I constantly proclaim myself the "king of the supercharged mode." As a result of the way I see life, eat, meditate, and exercise, my energy level is so high that, at times, it seems unfortunate that sleeping would be necessary with all the things I want to and feel like I should do. Nevertheless, the things that contribute the most to this *supercharged mode* are the big goals and motivations that I have for my life. Without them I wouldn't be talking about a supercharged mode, rather the frigid mode, a state characterized by low energy and a high level of mental and physical laziness. Low energy is one of the main causes of catching a disease. In the supercharged mode, in contrast, the best decisions in life are "cooked," risks are taken on, you go after everything with a strong attitude and determination.

The advantage of keeping up a supercharged mode, ambitious and full of energy, is that fire exorcizes beasts, scares them, and makes a winner of you.

I am going to give you a compelling example: I spoke to an elderly lady who told me: "Juan Diego, the problem is that computers and smartphones don't attract me, I wasn't born in the era when they were invented so that I could understand them and use them well." And I told her: "I can show you that this is false with a thirty-second example." She looked at me in shock and wondered how I was going to demonstrate that she could handle technology and could use it. "Do you have granddaughters or grandsons?" I asked. "Yes, Juan Diego, I have a granddaughter."

With this in mind, I said: "What would happen if that granddaughter went abroad to study and said to you, 'Grandma, I want to communicate with you over WhatsApp, Facebook, or Skype and tell you everything that is happening to me'?" I am sure that the affection, love, and happiness of being in contact with her would make you overcome your fear of technology and begin to use it, I told the lady. "Of course, Juan Diego, she said to me." The problem isn't the technology. The problem is that we often lack the motivations to overcome defects, fears, and develop our skills. The motivation in this case is to talk to the granddaughter. This brightens up her life, motivates her, it is something she is eager for, and it will end up getting her to use something she has stayed away from—technology.

There is a fascinating book entitled *The 33 Strategies of War*, by Robert Green, which talks a lot about Napoleon. It says that he spent entire days without sleep and he would say that he had so many things to do that he would forget his tiredness. You don't really get tired when you work a lot, rather you get tired when you don't enjoy what you are doing. Nothing produces more fatigue than a routine and boring life. So, if you have motivations, you will be likely to maintain a good attitude, you will be inclined to fill yourself with reasons to see things differently. You will see a half-full glass rather than a half-empty one. In a fascinating seminar I attended in the United States given by Anthony Robbins, I learned that in order to change the state of mind in which one is and go from unhappiness to joy, from depression to euphoria, from the frigid mode to supercharged mode, one had to change three things: language, approach, and physiology. With some winning words, a positive and optimistic approach, and an upright stance which included smiles and energy, you get results. With the opposite, your results will be different. Your state of mind determines your results. Don't forget it.

One often finds people who are very stubborn and obstinate and who believe that they have no motivations. Nothing, absolutely nothing moves them to do something to change their lives. I heard about a very famous story: a person who was going to commit suicide because there was no reason to live went to a psychiatrist, an expert in handling these types of cases. The person said, very sadly, but with confidence: "I don't have any reason to live." The psychiatrist said: "I agree with you, kill yourself!" The patient didn't expect him to say that. He changed instantly: "No, but how can I commit suicide if I have this and that" and he continued listing different things that gave him a reason to continue living. At times it is necessary to dive within ourselves, look very carefully at our surroundings and in our hearts to find the motivations, and if we don't see them, then build them. Blessed are those who are at the bottom of the well because they have nowhere to go but up.

Do you still don't know how to build a motivation? I'm going to tell you something useful: "Throw the cow over the cliff," Are you very unhappy with your current job? Quit. If you don't have the good luck I had to be laid off a job that I didn't enjoy, fire yourself. The next day you will be forced to think about what you are made of. You will have to figure out how to light that torch that is inside you, how to make it burn so brightly that they can see you coming from a distance, and go out and conquer the world. Your financial genius and entrepreneurial gene that we all have should come to the surface.

A case that illustrates this is the life of Michael Bloomberg. He was laid off from a prestigious firm on Wall Street and literally built an emporium based on Bloomberg, his financial information service company. Once he was asked how he had arrived at that state, to which he replied: "I got tired of sending out resumes in order to get a job. I couldn't get one so I had to set up Bloomberg." In other words, being laid off was one of the best things to happen in his life, just as it was for me.

If you don't enjoy what you do or "they throw your cow over the cliff," then, being laid off is your chance to find your lodestar, learn what you are made of, and finally, answer and tell yourself what you came into this world for. Let's look at a second example of what it is like to have the courage to face life. What do people usually ask when they are looking for a job? "How much will they pay me?" As Warren Buffett told Benjamin Graham: "I will work for you for free, give me a job with no pay."

This is what I translate colloquially as "following in someone's footsteps"—let me work beside you to learn. At first, Benjamin Graham, the father of financial analysis, didn't hire Warren Buffett because he was, according to him, overqualified for the position he wanted. But later they worked together, and Warren Buffett always considered Benjamin Graham his mentor, his tutor in financial matters.

"Doesn't it seem risky to you, Juan Diego, for me to quit my job when I'm paying my debts with my salary?" It seems more risky not to be happy!

These are two traditional examples of what a strong attitude is, two examples that teach us lessons. First: not crying, not getting depressed because you lost your job or decided to quit the one you have because it didn't match your "reason why" at all. And, second, not always accepting a job based on what they are going to pay you, but rather on how much you are going to learn there. They may pay very little or not pay anything, but what you learn will allow you to leverage, improve, and feed your knowledge so that afterwards, you won't even bother about a salary any more than Warren Buffett did at one time. I still remember as if it were yesterday how little I was paid as a university professor and after being laid off of a job that I didn't enjoy. It didn't matter to me. I knew that doing something that I liked such as research and teaching plus having more free time to write would bear fruit. So it did. Today, others who earned more than I did during my time at the university but doing something they weren't passionate about and and with no free time at all, not even for their family, earn much less than I do today, and when you ask them about their "reason why" or purpose in life, they remain silent or ask what that is.

It is clearer at this point that a strong attitude is the only sustainable competitive advantage that exists. People say that it is knowledge. That isn't true. What is known today could be obsolete tomorrow or be completely useless. But what is really vital in any period of life is the attitude, the "hunger," the determination, the constant desire to achieve things. Look at how hot you burn in the distance, how supercharged you are, how much of what is inside you is reflected on the outside. Look at whether or not you are a burning torch that gives rise to Level 10 motivations, to macro objectives, to transcending, to see if you are a purple cow that literally eats the world with your attitude. We already talked about being extraordinary, about discovering that other being that you may have sleeping inside there. When you have this attitude, thousands of good things happen in your life—take better advantage of them! Remember that when the day is spoiled, it isn't because the sky turned gray but rather because you don't know what to do with that climate.

When the Universe sees that you'll rise to the challenge (in mindset, knowledge and attitude), it takes a picture and concludes: I'll give it to you!

Habits are very important in all of this. Having a good attitude always has to do with not being inconsistent. There are people who consult me and tell me that their financial health is not good, and they constantly have money problems. I begin with the person by looking at their habits and discover, for example, that almost all the accounts they follow on Twitter, if they have it, are show business gossip. There is nothing wrong with that at all. It is to be respected even if I don't share it, but with respect to financial and pro-wealth habits, you have to go beyond your taste for certain things. You need to think about what it takes to really grow as a person and produce a better performance.

It is vital, therefore, to be consistent, goal-oriented. I need money, I follow accounts that provide for this purpose. But there are people, to continue with the examples, who are focused on soccer accounts though they have no desire to be soccer players. I love soccer, but I follow very few soccer accounts because that isn't my interest; soccer's not my life. So, one thing is what I like and another thing is what I need. Be consistent: that way my habit will further the accomplishment of the objective. This is vital and a clear mindset helps do that. I want something, therefore I act accordingly, this is an essential part of cultivating and having a good attitude.

When you are able to master that inner voice that limits and paralyzes you, you become the captain of your life and master of your destiny.

In chapter 2, I spoke of "Matilda," that inner voice which must be fought and silenced because it is always torpedoing our projects and dreams. That is the voice of fear, of the education we receive that cuts our wings. It is the voice of all the white and black cows that are part of the crowd and who are shocked to see anyone who differentiates himself and wants to change his environment through his determination. "Matilda," or whatever you'd like to call it, is there, and we need to eradicate it. Achieving that is also a matter of attitude.

Modifying the behaviors or habits that prevent you from being rich has to do with defeating that voice that tells you: "You should do this because you have always done it that way, do it because everyone does it, don't look for another way because it is easier this way." Attitude is mastering yourself, doing things that you are afraid to do like walking on fire. Attitude is feeling and believing very firmly that you're able to do much more than you have already done.

"What do you mean, walking on fire, Juan Diego"? My experience of a life transformation through the NLP led me to do it, literally, when I faced that test, and the photo of that moment is on Twitter. There were coals at 800°C in front of me, and I stepped out to go first after stoking the fire with industrial alcohol. Why do I recall that moment? Because Matilda appeared, and said: "You got burned by a hot coal jogging down the beach a few years ago. Do you want to burn yourself again?" Matilda wants me to lose heart, stay behind, and make no progress, to never know my limits, to continue to remain the same.

But the prize, the treasure, was huge. I had a coach at that time who helped me to pass that test with good training prior to it, and he made me see that when I reached the other side I would feel like I could take the world by storm. This is an expression that I really like as you have already seen, and it means to be able to do anything, to eradicate any vestige of fear. Said and done: I walked on fire, achieved the goal, and I felt like Superman. And Matilda? Fine, thanks. I didn't see her anywhere. What do I want to make clear here? That we are governed to a greater or lesser degree by that small inner voice, that limiting voice, and silencing it with our attitude is mandatory.

I'd like to ask you this question: Have you achieved what you want in life yet? The answer most certainly is "no," and when the reasons for this are analyzed, the guilty party will be shown to be that little voice that has, over the years, stopped you from taking the risk of changing your environment and reality and using another language (remember what we said about language and its importance) to set forth your dreams, your "reason why," and what you project for your life another way.

It is the responsibility of each one of you if you want to be rich or not, and make yourself better or eradicate "Matilda". Call it whatever you want. It is the voice of labels and tombstones that says, "I am afraid," "I don't deserve it," "this isn't going to work," "what can I expect with this kind of education," "I can't change," "I'm fine here," and so on with an endless number of excuses. The following is the specific question you need to ask yourself: Is Matilda bigger than my dreams? Am I the captain of this ship which Matilda is in? Is she a mere stowaway who must leave?

The conversation you have had with yourself about why you haven't achieved what you want is what explains why you haven't achieved it. The solution? Divorce yourself from that history and build a new one. And there a strong attitude has the leading role.

7

HOW TO START

There are many people who approach Invertir Mejor and come to my conferences because they have the desire to start their own business. However, it's possible that they're still not clear on what to do, or sometimes they have the ideas to set up a business, but don't take the required steps to achieve that and become successful.

I think that the entrepreneur has characteristics that are in his DNA. For example, he is usually a person with a lot of initiative, ideas, and a lot of energy; a person who likes challenges, is given to taking on risks, and, to put it colloquially, is a go-getter. However, the definition of an entrepreneur that I like the best is the following: an entrepreneur is the person who sees an opportunity where many others see a problem. He leverages a situation to start and set up a business and becomes successful.

However, there are people who say that they weren't born to start a business, but oddly enough, they have never given themselves the chance to do it. So, how do they know they weren't born to be entrepreneurs? They have preferred to work, like the majority, at a job they don't enjoy, that allows them little time to see their family, and which pays them poorly—just enough to be able to meet their debts and limit themselves to surviving. That is not the life I want for you, and I'm sure that it isn't the one you want either.

Of course, there are also many people who have started a business, who stepped into the ring, but repented of having done it because they ran into a huge number of obstacles that prevented them from achieving what they wanted and chose to give up. It is understandable because it isn't always a bed of roses. We've already seen that these life decisions like wanting to be rich and changing our current financial situation require great determination and will. It means to go into a special mode, the purple mode, the supercharged mode as I have called it, and there is no going back on that. We are going to give suggestions on how not to die in the attempt, how not to lose heart on the road to becoming an entrepreneur and changing our level of income.

It's not just a matter of having an idea; there are many ideas. It's an idea that resonates with you; an idea to push ahead with and one that you have to feed on a daily basis. It's like a seed that we want to see germinate and that must be watered and cared for. Also, the idea must be financed and, most importantly, it must be defended.

Many people think that the major limitation to starting a business lies in the lack of money, but that's not the main difficulty. The most difficult thing is to live with those who tell you: "That's not going to work. Why are you going to get involved in that project? You will lose money on it." What is worse is that many times these enemies of launching a business are members of our own family, friends, and the very demons you, the entrepreneur, have in your own mind.

I argue the following: if a person is not able to overcome the scepticism of his family; if a person is not able to prevail over the doubts of his friends and, I repeat, his inner demons that encourage him to surrender, that person is literally not an entrepreneur. The majority of processes of entrepreneurship that arise do not reach port and are unsuccessful. But the question we have to ask ourselves is: are we going to let ourselves be intimidated by those statistics or, as I always say, are we going to try to be in that small percentage of the population that is entrepreneurial and that does become successful?

I do an exercise when I have personalized sessions with my Purple, Gold and Elite partners in Invertir Mejor. I tell them the following: if I could finance a business for you, if I provided the capital, what business would you start? Two things happen. The first is that they say, "I can't think of anything in particular, I have no ideas." And second, the idea they have is usually very generic and vague. What do you gain by saying, "I want to start a entrepreneurial undertaking that will allow me to have a company that reduces pollution"? Very little. I don't mean to say that the concern about reducing pollution isn't important; rather, it is very general and abstract. But if I train you, make demands of you, if I play the role of devil's advocate because you also need someone to question you and I say: "bring your response down to earth; make it more specific," the majority hesitate and remain silent.

It is vital to have an idea that has to do with what you like, that there is a demand for in the market, and with which you can do things better than the rest, but I repeat: bringing it down to earth is essential in the process of entrepreneurship. Don't start a business just because you had an idea or think that you had an inspiration. It is, of course, very important for you to enjoy it and that you are passionate about it to the point that it is the only thing you think about, but create a work team who will ask you questions, who will ask about your "reason" for doing it and also "how" you are going to do it. This helps a lot in the process. "How are you going to finance it?, who are you going surround yourself with?, what are your advantages for getting this project off the ground?, have you analyzed the competition?, haven't you seen all the companies that offer the same service?" are questions that the people who really want to contribute to your project have in mind and it is good to listen in order to reaffirm the path you are going to start down.

Then, and using the example above, create the company to help reduce pollution or whatever the idea is that occurs to you, but make sure that the "reason why" you are creating it is clear. Is it to become a millionaire? That's not bad, but we have already mentioned the absolute necessity of having transcendental reasons that motivate our actions, Level 10 motivations, the highest ones we can imagine and that go beyond the idea of having a lot of money. "I am going to create a company that will reduce environmental pollution in order to generate better health conditions for more people in my city through the use of cleaner energy sources" and, based on that better definition, you are sure to find the financial resources to get your business going.

I can't live without Level 10 motivations; they allow me to live by doing what I love, while others survive by doing what they hate.

There are people who go aimlessly back and forth, lost. Today you see them working on one thing and in six months, another and they make no progress on any of them. The reason is that they made the following three errors: first, they didn't do what they do best; second, they didn't check out the market demands. Do people need your product, what you sell, produce, or distribute? And, third: Do you know how to do what you do better than the rest? If you concentrate on what you know how to do best, on what you like to do the most, and that people buy, you will reduce your chance of failing.

Let's look, for a moment, at one of the most common excuses of those who don't want to start a business: lack of money and resources to start up. "I have no money, so how am I going to be able to start my business?" Even worse, they say: "Of course, look at that person. I'll bet he has money because he was born with a silver spoon in his mouth. He was able to set up his company even though my idea is still better than his." Or they cling to other types of excuses such as: "I couldn't set up my company because I am too young, I'm too old, I'm a woman, I have a lot of obligations, I'm ugly, I'm too skinny, I don't know people," and so it goes with a super long list of reasons for not even beginning to change and fight for their dreams. But, of course, when they see other people who were able to increase their income, they look at them with resentment, envy, and even hatred.

Let's go back to the subject of money. First: currently, to finance your projects, you can get interest rates that are lower than those that existed years ago not only in the region but also in the world. Second: There are more and more entities responsible for sponsoring processes of entrepreneurship. There are angel investors across the globe, people who are willing to provide capital, act as partners of your idea and the entrepreneurial project and in that capacity, receive future earnings. In addition, there are also venture capital funds that can leverage your project. I think that the financial obstacle is surmountable as long as you have an idea, a good work team and a lot of stubbornness and perseverance. Invertir Mejor, my company, a successful entrepreneurship project, didn't require financing from a bank nor contributions of partners. I always had one thing clear: if the idea is good, the capital will look for it and the capital arrived. All it took was a few seminars on investing over the Internet for non-experts in order to obtain the resources that made it possible for my company to start growing. "If you want something, go get it. Period.", as the saying goes.

> **Pleasure is what I feel when I see so many people—those wich nobody believed in, not even their families—making progress and becoming purple.**

The question that arises then is, how can I generate business ideas? You may not have the capital right now, but if you have the idea and it is your passion, capital will come. If, on the other hand, you have the capital, but there are no ideas, capital will fade away. There are people who say to me: "No ideas come to me. What can I do to become much more creative, to identify business ideas? In other words, what can

I do to get that light bulb to go off, to rub that lamp and get that Aladdin that we all have inside to come out?"

Regarding this, I think that the majority of people don't face pressing needs the way they should and due to that nothing occurs to them. How is something going to occur to them, I ask, if they don't have any pressing needs that urge them to create and search for new alternatives? In other words, comfort is an attack on financial progress, an attack on generating ideas. It is the down payment to being poor and remaining anchored to a job that we don't enjoy. There is something fundamental, especially for young people, and that is to become independent. It is necessary to make the leap from living with your parents to living alone as quickly as possible. The more you face pressing needs, the more you reject having everything done for you, the more you assume responsibilities, the more you will progress from a financial point of view. Of course, it is very important to spend time with and enjoy your family. There is nothing more edifying than that. But when you remain with your family so long, when it is so comfortable, when you are so afraid of separating yourself from them, when you want them to do everything for you, iron your clothes, serve you a hot meal, make your bed, and the rest of the amenities you have when you live in your parents' house, you are avoiding responsibilities at a high price. In other words, it defers your progress. The price of comfort, the price of security is called the non-achievement of wealth. I'll say it a thousand times. One of the things that is conducive to not generating ideas is that we literally don't need them because we are in a comfort zone in which everything is done for us and no demands are made. We are stuck there content with the status quo, very comfortable, but I repeat, at the cost of putting off our success.

The comfort zone is too small for anyone to become great within it.

My first successful process of entrepreneurship was in 2004 and I did it with savings that I had been gathering as a university professor along with my income from seminars. As you can imagine, they were very small. However, when the idea is good, the resources appear, as I mentioned. If an idea is attractive enough, it doesn't require a lot of infrastructure, a lot of capital, nor many fixed costs for you to begin to generate fruit within a short period of time. So, I think that the obstacle of money has to be overcome, and it cannot be anything that blights the idea of the entrepreneur in the least.

I saw a very clear opportunity. At that time there were increasingly more people buying a personal computer and, at the same time, dissatisfaction with traditional investments was growing: the CDs (Certificates of Deposit), bonds, savings accounts, and the rest of the alternatives that offered very low interest rates. So what did I do? I put together those two points—trends and dissatisfaction—and I showed people how they could invest differently through that computer they had recently purchased but were not using of nor making money with but, rather they were simply keeping it on a desk in a room as if it were a flower vase. A need arose and I created a product that satisfied it. That is where the raw material of the entrepreneur is. The entrepreneur wasn't born to complain, he wasn't born to cry, he was born to sell handkerchiefs while others cried. Selling handkerchiefs is where the capital is, not in the tears shed.

You have to analyze many things of course: the context and the need that you want to meet, the competition, your differentiating factor, that personal stamp, and why they are going to choose your product or service instead of another. In particular, review what is called the state of the art when you are going to set up your business. Look at what there is very carefully, not just what the people need but who is meeting those needs and how. An idea may occur to you that you can create a business with, but at the same time, there are many companies that produce or distribute the same thing that you have in mind and better than yours. Give added value with the something extra that causes them to buy from you and not from another. In addition to this, I will give these suggestions: the first is not to load up on fixed costs, rather keep them at bay because there are people who start with inflated expenses including a very large infrastructure, hiring many people and setting up huge, luxurious offices only to realize two months later that they cannot go on. They went broke. Don't load yourself with fixed costs, please.

I tell the participants of my financial freedom and personal finance seminary: I didn't come here to tell you that you have to set up a hot dog stand, a car dealership, a lamp factory, or a gas station, whatever, no, no, no. I can't impose that. You have to find that which you like to do, the thing that you do better than anyone else, and that is a need to be satisfied. This need to satisfy is often found through observation. In order to create my own business, what do I see in the market, on the social networks? What are people asking for? What do people need? They say that where someone sees an insoluble problem, the entrepreneur sees a business opportunity. And that is true.

Keep saying that it's too difficult to get money and it'll become reality. Keep saying that you were born to live in abundance and so it shall be.

There are also some who say to me, as an excuse for not launching out, things like this: "I can't think of anything" or "everything has already been invented." As I converse with these people and probe into their daily habits, I discover that they don't read anything or read as little as possible. They talk to very few people who have progressed financially. They don't have good role models. They spend their time watching irrelevant TV programs. They don't subscribe to any successful publication and, therefore, the messages they are sending to their brains are not useful. And on top of all of that, they don't know what their "reason why" is or they lack of transcendent goals or Level 10 motivations. Because of that, I understand why they are so unlikely to be able to think of anything useful and, therefore, cannot get a business off the ground for example.

The second is to see if the product is in demand, to see if there is a felt need you can provide for in the milieu, or if there is an advantage for you in supplying a better service than others. It's one thing to take the risk of starting a new business and another thing to tackle becoming self-employed. These are two very different things.

Third, make this product or this service known to the largest number of people you can and to do that, the suggestion is to leverage this wonder called the Internet. People need to see what you do and promise. We are faced with a visual generation that focuses on what is going viral. Don't write so much; demonstrate. Everything is very visual due to lack of time. Consumption of videos is growing and while one person looks at a text message, many more will look at a text with a photo. Let your product talk when they see it. If it is a service, let the testimonies and results speak for it. "I don't have a product to sell." Perhaps you are wrong: You are a product, remember that.

People need your business to be on the Internet. That is where they will look, buy and where they spend much of the day. How many of them does your product reach? Is your business on the Internet? Or do you only have an email address? You can no longer say that you don't like to sell. If you don't sell, you don't eat; if you don't eat, you die.

How do I develop a business idea?
Three questions in detail

» *What do I like to do.* Don't focus on what you lack to set up a business, but on what you have to set it up. Don't tell me what you don't like. Tell me instead what moves you, what you're passionate about. Your strengths should be related to that "reason why" you came into this world, and you should invest in them.

» *What do I do better than others.* Find out the state of the art. Ask Dr. Google who does what you want to do, how they do it, and print your seal and put a pretty little bow on it. The packaging, as Steve Jobs said, is what matters.

» *What need is there that I can meet.* People need you to save them time and improve their quality of life. Don't hesitate to do anything that makes the buyer's life easier. Why has the mobile phone been a sales success in recent decades? Because it makes life easier. Today, the telephone allows me to pay for a utilities and public services, communicate with my entire team over WhatsApp, and buy on the main German stock market index without ever leaving my home or office. There are more mobile phones than people in the world. You don't have to compete with Apple or Samsung; just incorporate the essence of what I am saying into your business.

And, fourth, a very important point concerning processes of entrepreneurship is to surround yourself with a good work team. I want to pause here a moment on this key aspect because the entrepreneur needs people who are going down the same road he is. This is a kind of self-criticism that I have been trying to master over time. For me it was very hard to delegate. If we use soccer as an example, we could say that I was one of those guys who take a corner kick and then, also want to go after the ball to head it. I was the messenger/gofer, general director, finance manager, assistant as well as the one who generated the content for Invertir Mejor on the social networks and on top of that the promoter, and commercial executive. I did everything, and that is a huge error because no matter how passionate you are about what you are doing, the day will still only have 24 hours, and we have to accept the fact that we can't do everything.

Your mindset and habits define your assets. One good habit is to surround yourself with people who are excited about your idea and build on it; avoid toxic people.

You have to delegate, you need to create a team with several disciplines: for example, one person who is strong in programming, another in design, another to handle the area of accounting and taxes, others in social networks and in the marketing area so that you can dedicate your time to what you can actually do better than the others. If you concentrate on the work that really produces value and at the same time, let the others focus on what they do best, you will be multiplying your income and, thus, your business will be much more successful.

Your work group will allow you to clone yourself virtually. What does that mean? Have your products on the Internet. The generation of an entrepreneur's income cannot always require their physical presence. You can get sick, you will likely want to go on vacation or rest at some point in your life. Is there a team that can take your place when you aren't there? Avoid what happens to many companies where the business dies when the head dies. This interdisciplinary group which, I repeat, supplements what you don't know how to do is vital and makes it possible to clone yourself, to be on the Internet and thus make the generation of income automatic. This is essential for an entrepreneur. You cannot nor should do everything.

With it you are overcoming another barrier that some aspiring entrepreneurs see as a reason to give up: time. First, they say that they don't have the money. After that they say they don't have the time to build their business, whether this is because they are employed and the thought of abandoning the security of receiving a monthly salary or finding themselves forced to invest their hours of rest in building their business panics them. If you clone yourself virtually and keep up that habit, time will become an ally because even while you are sleeping or engaged in other activities, technology is doing the work for you. This is the case in my company. It is necessary to enjoy what you do, but always be focused on the fact that money and technology have to work harder than you do. Don't work to get more money but to reach the point where that money is working by itself and generating more money without meaning that you have to double or triple the time you devote to work. If you always think that you have to constantly work harder without money and technology working at the same time, you are working to receive a payment rather than the passive income of which we have already spoken.

To stimulate the genius and creativity of the people I work with, I think it is essential to pay them on the basis of their results. The average person conforms and likes to be comfortable. Paying based on what they produce develops the sense of urgency and your employees will demonstrate what they are made of. When you make demands of them, it encourages them to perform at their best, to become increasingly more intelligent, and I am sure that they will have a lot more creativity at the service of a cause.

Forget about your salary. The financial obsession of purple cows is passive income.

A final, necessary comment at this point: it is important to delegate, but do so with a work team that goes along with your thinking and ideals and that shares your vision. At Invertir Mejor, we are particularly rigorous about hiring people, and we tell the psychologist who interviews them to keep in mind certain qualities that we have to preserve. One of them is that we require people with lots of energy and passion for what they do. Someone for whom sleeping is a hobby cannot work on our team. Thus, the business owner must think about people who are as excited and motivated as he is about the original idea and the ones that emerge, but who themselves have a lot of personal motivations and pressing needs to create more and more income for themselves.

If you are very good at what you do and are part of the team of a new venture, you need have no fear of being paid based your results. When you have no confidence in what you do, you will always prefer to be paid by the hour, while if you are confident of what you do, and are also passionate about new ideas, you know that you can make a difference compared to other employees. High pressure turns coal into diamonds. A good employee, as a good investor, is like gold: he is refined by fire. Avoid jobs where you aren't under pressure if you really want to make progress in life. And if you're going to have employees, have ones who share this vigor with you.

Remember that starting a business venture and being financially independent will make more sense if you have a favorable impact on millions of people. I assure you that the same thing will also be true of the millions that go into your pocket.

8

THE STATE OF MIND AND WEALTH: THE HABIT OF THE SUPERCHARGED MODE

The state in which we find ourselves determines our results. We human beings are a sea of emotions, feelings and moods based on circumstances. This has an impact on wealth and our ability to acquire it. The state of mind controls the quality of your life. My partners in Invertir Mejor and those who have attended our seminars and conferences know that I love the supercharged mode, the name I have for the energy that moves me all the time, which has been, is, and I hope will be my predominant state of mind. In the supercharged mode, I have "cooked" the best decisions in my life. In the supercharged mode, I am more inspired and apt to develop ideas, tweets, and successful messages. In the supercharged mode, I also get sick less, I attract more abundance, and I become a magnet.

I want people to look at the future with optimism, feel fulfilled and full of energy all the time with the attitude, language and mindset to eat the planet and their dreams. That is the supercharged mode; that is the life of a purple person. However, there are people who, even though this almost spiritual state of mind attracts them, say: "It is very easy to talk about supercharged mode, Juan Diego; however, with all the problems I have, or with the difficult past I have, or this complex reality that surrounds me, how can I be in a supercharged mode?" We are going to shed some light on this and offer some keys to becoming rich, to becoming someone who is prosperous in every sense.

I want to show how a state of excitement, happiness, optimism, energy, will determine your results. Point number one, low energy is the main source of disease. Point number two, being depressed—what is going to happen?—Do you know any entrepreneur who is depressed? Up to this point, I haven't met a single person who has told me that while being in that kind of mood, an idea came to mind about setting up this or that company, starting a new business, or investing in something interesting and profitable. No, no, no, on the contrary, you have to help a person who is depressed, you have to change his mood, nothing will occur to us when we are depressed.

So when you do or stop doing things that have to do with the state you are in, a purple state, a state of being supercharged, a positive state, or a state of energy, I repeat, helps you carry out many activities. You jump, leap, move, and you want to start new projects. But a state of low energy or frigid mode as I have baptized it, a mood of " of "Nothing has changed. I guess I'm OK so don't worry about me." That attitude can be perceived and it's not helpful. It is a mood that acts as a repellent. It pushes people away, they don't like you. Think about the following: What do you feel when an ordinary person, not someone from your family or your best friend, begins to talk to you about diseases and problems, about how tired or sad he is. We can't wait to get out of there, to get away, and if our education and manners did not prohibit this, we would say, I don't give a rip, stop complaining right now, there are many with more problems than you have who don't complain and yet make progress. Don't talk to just anyone about your problems. They won't matter to some, others will be happy you have them, and for others this, will produce distrust. Do you want to fall into this state where instead of radiating energy, you only cause people to avoid you? I am sure that you don't. Otherwise you wouldn't be reading this book.

"And how do I change my state of mind, Juan Diego? How do I move to a supercharged mode, so that many good things happen to me?" To start with, let's lay out a worst case scenario: A person is in a bad state, he is in the pits, totally depressed. There are three specific suggestions for changing the mood we are in and they are language, approach, and physiology or body language. We give each a practical explanation.

> » **Language:** many people like us who are in a super-charged mode have a winner's language, and there are even words that we don't use in daily life. In contrast, when a person is at a low point with little energy, listen to him talk and you will see that, emotionally speaking, part of his negative mood revolves around the poor choices of words he uses. These are people who talk a lot about failure, how difficult the situation is, the diseases that they have suffered over the last year, the cost of living, the debts they have, how their husband or wife doesn't speak to them, the dog doesn't bark—and those are enough illustrations. What is more, the tone in which they speak is a very frail, weak, defeated tone of voice. Now you understand why they are that way. Language is a determining factor. The words and tone affect our future.

» **Approach:** there is a very simple sentence, repeated ad nauseam: "We see a half full glass or we see a half empty one." I have listened to people who say, "my life is a tragedy," and to that I say: rebuild your context. Granted, your life has been very hard, but you are still alive. Why not take advantage of that tragedy, as you call it, to teach many other people who may be in the same circumstances how to overcome them and start over? I am sure you haven't thought about it that way or were conscious of the ace card you had up your sleeve that would help you thrive. Those stories are the building blocks for the movie of your life. Whatever you have overcome, your experiences are not only something to remember; they're also something to share and sell. Yes, you read that correctly. Or is it that you don't want someone to tell you how to get what what you need, or how to overcome the difficulties that you are going through today? The approach is how I can see things through another lens and rebuild my state of mind. Now you see a half-full glass, when before you saw only a half-empty one.

» **Physiology or body language:** There are compelling figures on this: words are 7% of language or of the message; the tone is 38% of it, and 55% of your communication is physiology, as you already know. How much you smile, how straight your shoulders are, your gaze, how you move your hands. There are people with such a strong attitude that it leaves us perplexed, without words. They are iron-willed, positive, evolved. I want to meet these people. In contrast, there are other people who are seem to be jinxed, and so negative that we say, "don't even introduce them to me, I'm already getting a short circuit; I felt horrible energy; if I touch them, it will make me poor." Sound familiar? Perhaps a person like that went through your head. The physiology is *very important*. Look for example at how someone shakes your hand when you are introduced; how he walks. A person who walks along with his shoulders slumped over and looking down at the ground is already talking about himself and his expectations. There are people who come into my office for personalized sessions and—pay attention to this—before sitting down, I do an initial scan. After that I ask them if they will let me tell them what they are like. "What do you mean, Juan Diego, you don't even know me," they ask. "I just arrived and we haven't even begun to talk." In response to this, I tell them that I may be wrong, but that I can describe their virtues and defects with a high degree of accuracy. And I start to tell them, bluntly, what impression they gave me. The surprise that they feel when I describe things that they believed were very personal and not that evident with a high degree of accuracy is amazing. They look at me as if they are trying to wrap their brain around what I said and ask: "How do you know that I am like that?" I'm not a seer. What has actually happened is that they shake my hand weakly, look downward, and they also talk so softly that I can't even hear them. They are already talking and sending a message that certainly doesn't match the one they want and need to send. Be careful with that. Something very different occurs when I see people who are secure, look me in the eye, smile openly, who are concerned with how they dress, who walk with pride and without fear; people who have fire in their belly.

There is no doubt that many people will insist that their lives are full of problems and, therefore, they can't be happy. So, how are they going to improve their state of mind when their life is so burdened. There is, however, no direct relationship between problems and happiness. There are many people who have many problems and are happy. And there are others who don't have any problems but are unhappy. What is more, they have a unique ability to invent problems and create difficult situations for themselves, and that's not the way it should be.

On top of that they say to me, "How am I not going to be depressed with all the problems I have?" Ask yourself the following questions: Will being depressed solve your problems? The answer is no. So I firmly think that the consequence of that energy, that attitude that supercharged mode, that desire to fly will change your reality. If you change what you are, you change what you do. How do you change what you are? You cannot achieve that just by sending more information to the brain or just going through exciting experiences. You also have to maintain a high state of energy, an emotional state that is always better, that attracts, that summons, that is provocative and irresistible. You are not what you do in life. You are what you awaken in others. There are people who are pure, flowing energy, people you want to touch in hopes that some of it sticks to you. We know that there are others who don't attract anything but bad stuff, because of the bad energy they have.

From now on, behave as the person you will be; don't wait until you become that person. It'll be very useful.

A practical recommendation for keeping your spirits up: detoxify yourself from bad news. We worry a lot about what we eat because we want to look good. You should also be concerned about what you listen to, what you read, what you see, what you talk about if you want to change your state of mind. Several years ago I stopped watching the traditional TV newscasts which seemed more like court reports. They only talk about robberies, rapes, kidnappings, and extortions. After watching them, you feel depressed and hopeless. They were showing me a partial reality as if it were the total one, most likely because good news don't sell very well. I stopped watching them. I spend that time reading, listening to good music, playing sports, or spending time with my family. Nothing toxic. Get thee behind me, Satan.

So remember the three key things for changing a state of mind: language, approach, and physiology. And as a healthy habit, avoid bad news and toxic people as much as possible. A pessimist who has never been able to fulfill his dreams is not the best counselor for you to fulfill yours. So stay as far away from people like that as you can.

Sometimes with certain people I opt for silence and distance and they ask me, why are you so quiet?, and I say: "I'm waiting for us to change the topic." "Did you hear that someone lost their job? Did you hear that so-and-so died? Guess who was diagnosed with a terminal illness," and I say: When are you going to bring me good news? When are you going to talk about possibilities that exist? When are you going to see a half-full glass? This may even happen with people who are close to you, but to be wealthy, we need different types of messages. We love our families, but if they only talk about negative things, we have to choose between whether we want that (poverty) or prefer inspiration from and interaction with people who share our dreams, who are pointed in the same direction, who have big, noble, far-reaching, and inspiring goals.

Likewise, when someone tells you that things are very difficult and that there is no future anywhere because they have seen that on TV, turn a deaf ear to that and choose to think about the new opportunity that your present and future give you all the time. It doesn't matter what the situation is in a country and its economy, you forge your own destiny with your attitude and talent. When I decided to avoid the news on TV and radio, I began to have more conversations with people who could provide me with positive energy and knowledge. I readjusted my surroundings and continued to make quantum jumps.

"How do you take quantum jumps, Juan Diego?" Live quantum experiences such as reading books and getting to know extraordinary people that make you say: WOW!

Emotional experiences are the ones that produce the most profound and long-lasting changes. Let me tell you something: dedicate more time to your family since you could lose a loved one at any time—your mom, your dad, who knows? And you may think that our time in this world is truly very short and that they need you to be with them more. But the next day you may forget and what you share with them will remain limited. In contrast, if I tell you, "your mom is in intensive care and you have to go to the hospital right now," I'm sure you won't hesitate but will leave immediately to visit her and be with her because there is a real possibility you will never see her again. Then your attitude really would change, and if she survives, you will continue to devote much more time to her. The reaction is completely different, and what is most important is what you will do from now on. That is the difference between a rational experience based on information and an emotional one that is lived and felt.

Why do emotional experiences have a greater impact than the rational ones? Because, in the first example, what happens to my family doesn't become a priority based on the information I have. In contrast, in the second case, there is a very strong emotional shock that immediately locks in an intense need to continue dedicating more time to your mom since you have FELT the reality that she could die at any moment.

Let's take advantage of this to remember another aspect that has to do with the good or bad that we surround ourselves with. If you really want to be rich and change your financial habits, think very carefully about the people who surround you. Those who have a poor mindset are unlikely to become wealthy, and if their friends are poor and don't want to escape that, it will certainly be easier for them to stay that way. I'm not telling you to abandon your friends or choose them by how much money they have, but it would be useful if, at least the majority of them or, at a minimum, those you spend the most time with wanted to make progress, had an abundance mindset, and shared dreams with you. It has been proven that a person's income is similar to the average earnings of their five closest friends. Therefore, if those five friends have poor mindsets and earnings, you run the risk of catching that from them and their lack of aspirations, their dismal energy, and their low altitude thinking when what you want is to fly high.

For me, material things do matter. With this book, I hope to make you see the connection that exists between your mood, a winning mindset, and the things that you get. Having luxuries doesn't make us better people. That is clear, but the following is also clear: the good life is the good life while the bad life isn't life. We didn't come into this world to just survive. We came to live and I'm not talking about just the clothing, jewelry, trips, or cars type of luxury. This also refers to sending your children to the best schools, the chance to attend the best universities, to have the best life insurance, and the most comprehensive health plan. That is also what I'm referring to with the words live and not survive.

How can someone become a millionaire if, when asked what he thinks about money, he says: "It's a necessary evil."

When we buy luxuries we send ourselves a message: if I bought this luxury, I was telling the Universe that I will have the where-with-all to pay for it, and I deserve it. When I abstain from buying it, the message is different: that it is for someone else. I cannot make that purchase, and it is unlikely that I can get the money to pay for it. These are two opposing emotions: deserve or not deserve, and they arise from different states of mind. What I want is for you to live the life of the minority who are the ones that earn the most income (remember: 10% of the world's population holds 90% of the wealth), to stop buying imitations or knock offs, but rather buy yourself the true luxuries you were born for and don't hesitate to do that.

I have always embraced the following thinking: you cannot wait until you are reincarnated to indulge yourself. We have to think about the fact that we are living the only life that we are going to live, and as a result, live it to the full. Today I don't have the money, but today will be over in a few hours. Tomorrow will be another day and the message I am sending is "I need resources to pay for that luxury that I just got for myself" and that message begins to work: ideas blossom and the business deals come. But if I abstain from making any purchase because "that's not for me, it's for someone else," what message am I sending myself? A white cow message of fear. I don't move, I am paralyzed, I don't buy anything. I'm not defending wastefulness here, because that's not the point either. I'm underlining the fact that, as I've already said, there is huge difference between living life and surviving, between buying what we deserve and buying what we have to.

Poverty mindset + poor literature + no wealthy friends = poverty mode.

If the motivation is strong as we have already seen, there is no valid excuse. There are two ways to get access to those luxuries if we want to talk about specifics: the first is to create assets. Make your business, or what you do best in life and the area where you are harnessing your talents to the fullest pay for the luxuries. We can also call that building an asset or a series of assets to pay for my luxuries, and as a result of it, I won't be interested in buying that lower priced car because it is the one that I can afford right now but rather the car of my dreams, the one that gives us a feeling of pleasure when we drive; that makes us soar and feel alive. Furthermore, what we put on to cover our bodies will no longer be rags or cloths; rather, we will dress the way we like and wear the best brands and high quality clothing. If you see it that way, it completely changes everything. This has nothing to do with you being a better or worse person due to the assets you have but, what a pleasure it is to be able to give yourself the luxuries that you want!

Mental programming is decisive, how I sell myself the ideas, how I assimilate the information that will change my life from not only the point of view of money, but also the viewpoint of my mindset, spirituality, and emotional intelligence. This mental programming, of course, has to do with all of the NPL topics and with how we are able to transform our reality based on what we think about.

I have known people who have confessed that they are deeply resentful of and even hate the rich despite the fact that those emotions are so strong and negative. On one hand, they want to be rich and be financially educated in order to obtain a higher income; on the other, they despise the rich, and if one goes by them, an endless list of insults and unpleasant adjectives describing that person begin to flow through their minds. Let's see, do you hate the rich because you are poor? Or are you poor because you hate the rich? How are you going to manage to become something that you hate? If you see a Ferrari or any other luxury car go by, do you think of all sorts of insults or do you say, "I will have a car like that" to yourself? These are very different ways to see the same event. So if I fill myself with resentment and criticize the thing that, deep inside, I am looking for, I will never obtain it since I am sabotaging myself all the time. You should, in contrast, embrace that desire so that it becomes a reality and be full of energy and a positive state of mind in order to build your road towards that goal. The greater the determination, the greater the degree of merit and the greater the reward.

Everything we have seen has to do with the essence of the "reason why" for their actions. The transcendental motive that drives you to seek new and higher income, your

Level 10 motivations, are the fruit of and can only be the fruit of energetic states of mind, your optimism, and conviction that you will achieve your dreams. When you talk about the purpose of your life, of the most important thing in your life even above your life itself, you have to have blood in your eye, fire and fireworks in your belly because to the extent that you talk the way you should, you will achieve what you want to be.

If, on the contrary, you demonstrate doubt, hesitation, or dithering on such a momentous topic, then that's not your "reason why." Not everyone has to find their "reason why" in life quickly. But when you think you have found it, do the following exercise: talk to your spouse or a close family member and tell them, "listen to me for 30 seconds while I talk to you about my 'reason why' since I think I have found it," and begin to talk. At the end ask: "How did that sound to you?" If your spouse says he saw magic, that he was infected with your enthusiasm, motivation, and the strength you infused into it, that is undoubtedly your "reason why" and you are on the right track. But if he has doubts about your proposal, this will be reflected in the language he uses, his physiology, tone of voice, in everything. If what you think is your "reason why" does not excite you nor get you out of the frigid mode you may have lived in for a long time, stop and rethink it.

I want the photo the Universe takes of you to transmit all that energy and enthusiasm of a "reason why" that is so transcendental, happy, and exciting that it infects everyone with their own supercharged mode and gives them much more vigor to devise more challenging goals. Don't forget that no matter how hard you may be working on great things, some day those things will look small. Careful! Don't stop with the first goals. Keep going. We often think we are doing remarkable things, but over time, new deeds put them in the shade. What message am I sending you? Non-conformist to the death. Look at who you are comparing yourself to. There are people who think they are rich because they earn a thousand dollars, but that is only because everyone in their neighborhood earns a hundred. You are the captain of your destiny and by leveraging a good attitude, positive states of mind, and an optimistic mindset, you will earn more merit every day on your way to abundance and prosperity.

9

ENERGY, YOUR AGE, AND WEALTH

—

Energy is not an esoteric or magical subject, nor is it a superstition. Energy has to do with your attitude and mindset, and it's not related to your age. There are old people who are 20 and young people who are 70. When they ask me what age I am, I reply "I don't know." And I don't know for one reason: The years I have lived don't matter to me that much but, the unknown years ahead of me do. In addition, at different times during the day, my age is different. I am 70 years old when I give advice, 25 when I start a business, and ten when I play with my children.

What does this mean? Simple: he who says he is only a certain age is denying possibilities. Of course, all of us have a date of birth, and therefore, we have lived x number of years. Nevertheless, when I say that someone is denying possibilities, I am referring to the fact that, in general, people believe that since they have lived a certain number of years, they no longer can nor should do certain things. Nothing could be further from the truth. Age is a state of mind.

There are people to whom you say, for example, jump, shout, sing, dance, put a red shoe on one foot and a green one on the other and go to work like that... and they get strange look on their faces and answer in a serious tone: No, Juan Diego, some one my age doesn't do things like that.

That is fine for someone younger, but at 45, I'm not going to do that kind of thing. They're afraid of looking ridiculous, afraid of what others will say, what might happen if they do something different. Discomfort makes them anxious, and perhaps they are afraid. These fears are the brakes on our lives and our fulfillment. And, of course, they are the ones that hold us back on our way to wealth. And it is worth saying that they're not limited to age. They also include the way we are. When asked what they are like, they usually say that they are serious or extroverts; risk-takers or fearful; patient or impatient, and so on. Again, when I am asked what I am like, I say: I don't know, it depends. I can be serious when I am solving a problem. But that seriousness does me no good at a nightclub. I can be elegant wearing a fine silk handkerchief in the pocket on my jacket, but that same elegance is no good on a beach. I can be rational and reflective when I meditate, but passionate and explosive at a conference. Do you see, my dear reader, why I find it hard to define myself? It all depends on the circumstances. Defining ourselves rigidly also takes away our possibilities.

Those who say they have only one age, in turn, are usually people whose mindset has stagnated and has become closed as if it had frozen over time. They think they are only x number of years old and, therefore, they can only behave in a certain way. They limit themselves, and that is when they age. They say, "I've already done my duty," "I don't have anything else to to pursue," "At my age, there is no chance of anything else." Apart from using poor language, they have very low energy.

What is my suggestion on this point? When they ask you about your age or you think about it, look at it as something mental. If they are asking you how old you are, tell them, "that depends on the moment I am living," or "it depends on what I am doing."

Let's assume that we see a 60- or 70-year-old man hand in hand with a younger woman—let's say about 25 or 30 years old. The first thing that comes to our mind is to judge him and label him a "dirty old man." Most people would say that, at this point, that man should be doing other things and, therefore, has no right to have a girlfriend who is much younger than he is. Why? Because that is what we have become accustomed to doing—labeling, judging, and writing people off, saying that because something has always been that way, it must continue to be that way. I see it differently.

Let's begin with the fact that, for me, a person who is 60 or 70 years old may still be a very young person. And second, who am I to judge? Judging is one of the worst investments that exists; it is terrible because it cannot improve either the one who judges nor the one who is judged. The one who judges is petty, and his hatred and ignorance gnaw at him. And, the one who is judged doesn't even realize that someone is judging him. At one time, I used the sharp insight I had to judge and label people. With the wisdom that the passing years have given me, I emphatically recommend: don't judge. It is, I repeat, a bad investment; a habit of the poor.

We think that the possibilities for growth are immense, infinite. Let's stop criticizing so much and concentrate on our energy, on making ourselves dynamic, on strengthening our mindset daily, and not on behaving the way we have been told that a person of one age or another should behave. Let's criticize less and perceive life more optimistically and be open to the possibilities. That is part of the supercharged mode that I like so much, a vital and tolerant mode. Don't label yourself because that way you are stripping options away. Don't tie a millstone around your neck. Remember what we have already seen—the immense ability human beings have to change and constantly improve.

The great advantage most people have is that if they subtract the years they have been *surviving* from their age, they become very young.

There is an international role model who has a great impact on me and that is Anthony Robbins, a legend in the world of transformation and leadership, someone who is almost 60 years old. In one of his seminars in the United States, which I attended, he began to speak at ten in the morning and stopped at two in the morning the following day; sixteen hours in a row, just as I said, without stopping, in pure supercharged mode, and I didn't even notice if he went to the bathroom during that time or if, like any other human being, he drank water. As I can attest, an extraordinary mindset, a healthy diet and exercise, and total passion for what he does stand out as the main reasons behind his stamina to go so long.

There will surely be more reasons. Absolute supercharged mode. A person without the mental, physical, and spiritual preparation or the urge to take the world by storm, like Anthony Robbins, will probably never manage to remain standing on a stage for half that time nor have the impact that he had on the attendees, and I include myself among them, even if that person is 20 years old. Lesson: physical age doesn't mean greater strength. Introduce me to someone who is 20 years old and can do that without the qualities I have already mentioned and I'll take my hat off to him. I would pay to see him. On top of all that, Anthony Robbins is a person who has a lot of money, but keeps his ambition intact, although you can see from afar that his 'reason why' goes far beyond material things. "Are you implying, Juan Diego, that a potent and transcendental 'reason why' invigorates and keeps one's energy high?" You should have no doubt about that. And that is why it is important to have it and to remember, at this point in time, the suggestions given in this book for those who haven't yet discovered it or for those who do have a clear "reason why" but don't tap into it. A purpose in life must be related to your strengths or to what you do best. It should motivate you to develop it to the point where it becomes your Level 10 motivation for life even above your family. Reading, pressing needs, and spirituality facilitate achieving it and, what is more, the Universe isn't indifferent to your incessant search. Your determination shows you are worthy to find it.

But, going back to the case of Mr. Robbins, there is more. The day after having talked with an inhuman degree of energy for sixteen consecutive hours, the session was given by one of his staff. He introduced himself to the audience. He had charisma and an incredible handling of the public, and also gave a very extensive presentation. What a surprise when he revealed that he was 62 years old! Everyone in the auditorium was stunned, and I realized again that it is not the age in years which defines a person, but rather the attitude, behavior, and mindset.

To make a long story short, one of my closest advisors, my father, was more than 70 at the time I was writing this book. He stays up to date, goes to bed late, gets up early, studies like nobody else, and never believed what many people are told long before they reach his age: "You already did your duty." That limiting message eats them alive. He, in contrast, remains in a supercharged mode that I haven't seen in younger people.

It is sad to see 20- and 30-year olds and realize very quickly that they have written themselves off. They became accustomed to many amenities that they didn't have to make much effort to get. They were born with a silver spoon in their mouths, and they don't value sacrifices and earning things with hard work. Analyze them and you will see pauper-like and stultified mindsets due to the fact that they're not eager to learn, create, or live more and differently; they don't have a "reason why," and it's obvious.

There are ways to increase and stimulate energy. For example, I sleep little, but I sleep well. Six hours of sleep are enough for me, if that sleep is unbroken and deep. Exercise at least three times a week. Find a place for reflection, meditation and silence. Listening to music (electronic music, in particular, when I want to raise my energy and rebuild my state of mind, and zen music when I want to meditate and relax) is decisive for maintaining my supercharged mode. Each person should find something that recharges his energy using criteria, information, and the determination to make sustainable changes in his life in order to attain something better.

Words are magic; they are light. Words won't be carried away by the wind; define your reality. Pay attention to the words you say and the ones said to you. Be purple.

A Level 10 motivation is a source of energy as we mentioned. A motivation that is so strong that when Monday arrives, you welcome it with good spirits and eagerness. The motivation to get up every day and live it intensely, to be the captain of your destiny. Not like others who open their eyes and say, "Horrors! Another day I have to go to work at a job I hate, and especially when it is Monday!"

We need a lot of energy to face the future, to create our present and make it successful. Without that which nourishes our body and mind in order to go after those goals that we set for ourselves, it will be much more difficult to become wealthy. Cultivate habits in your life that fill you with energy: nutrition, exercise, reading, discipline, whatever you think will support and is closely related to your pursuit of wealth.

High energy will help you have more passive income. Without vitality and creativity, there can be no new income that doesn't require your physical presence. We cannot cope with pressing needs when our energy is low, a condition that is the main cause of diseases. Focusing on the future with optimism does require a lot of energy. And to do so, revising our past requires a winning and optimistic mindset. Perhaps those who say that the past is unchangeable are right, at least in that the facts cannot be changed. What you can change is the way the facts are understood, interpreted, and you leverage them.

Remember that getting leverage means taking what seems to be an obstacle, some fear, comments intended to sink us, situations that seem hopeless and turning them into the pillars that sustain our determination to become wealthy. For many, the past is a heavy weight that blocks off any glimmer of future wealth and prosperity. In other words, the past is like a black hole that can swallow the energy that we may manage to channel for our personal and financial growth in the present. It can be a torpedo that strikes and sinks our motivations. For many people, the past is the greatest fear of all.

However, remember that it is never too late to have a happy past—be very aware of this. *It is never too late to have a happy past* means that even though the past has already past, it has already been lived, you can always change the way you see that past. There are people who tell me, "Juan Diego, the past hurts me, I am affected by my past." For example, there are people who think they had an unhappy childhood because they were bullied, or because no one at home believed in them, or because they experienced very serious domestic violence, or because they were very poor. This lack of confidence has permeated their adult life and seems to be a phantom that holds them back. I have heard, for example: "I lack confidence, I'm not able to believe in my dreams, and I even think many times that I don't deserve prosperity or wealth".

I would kill just to turn anybody that has been told that he's just average into a purple person. Their cause is mine.

We cannot change the facts, but we can change the way we give meaning to the past. Rather than punishing ourselves, rather than looking up to heaven and asking, "My God why did this happen to me?," let's reconstruct the context and ask instead: what reason was there for this to happen to me; perhaps, because of what happened to me, I can become the person I want to be; as a result of the fact that this happened to me I will be able to reinvent and leverage myself with that past and rebuild my present and future. This is a quantum leap in all its dimensions.

The past isn't equal to the future unless you continue to live in that past. It is good for giving insight in order to disengage from a negative view of your past and instead leverage yourself with it, nourish yourself from it to rebuild your context, your present and hence your future.

Here's an example of a real case: I remember once a woman, mother of two daughters, told me the following: "Juan Diego, I hate my husband and that corrodes me. It harms me, and keeps me in a state of hatred." I asked her why she hated him and she replied:

"My husband abandoned my daughters and me. He never met his obligations to us after that, and I had to work from dawn to dusk, and often from 6 o'clock in the morning until late at night without seeing my daughters to be able raise them. This was while that scoundrel was living the good life and not giving a penny in support. What can I do in order to be able to move forward and make quantum leaps like the ones you describe?"

I told her that the beginning of her solution was implicit in her words. I said:

"Why don't you rebuild your context instead? Look at things differently and instead of hating that person, which does neither you nor him any good, say, 'OK, so now you've left us. We'll see what happens'. And immediately turn that desertion, that pain into another stimulus, an additional motivation to succeed, into an authentic wake-up call to build a successful movie of your life so that, when he see you afterwards, he asks himself, 'Why did I abandon them?'

So, look at how you can change hatred, turn that hatred around and leverage it with the "shit you are eating." Tell that man: "Did you think that we wouldn't be able to make progress without you? Look at the results." That woman, based on the suggestion that I gave her to rebuild her context, what had happened to her, was able to see that it is possible to transform one's hatred into a reason to fight; a reason that would lead her to demonstrate what she was actually made of.

Nothing is sadder than the death of someone who is destined to fly but just walks.

Another example. One day in my office, a young dreamer and one with a purple mindset, said during a personalized session, "Juan Diego, the past is sabotaging me." A very strong phrase and more common than we believe. I asked him, why he thought that. "Juan Diego, they don't believe in me at home. They always saw me as a good-for-nothing, a dreamer. They kept telling me that I didn't do this or that thing well. This even resurfaces in my dreams, and every time I think about my aspirations, these voices that are so strong and so deeply rooted emerge and paralyze me. What do I do?"

The answer I gave him was, "leverage yourself with these doubts, show them that the size of their criticisms can never be greater than the size of your dreams and that sooner or later they will be asking themselves why they didn't believe in you." What I mean by that is that a purple, a person with an extraordinary mindset that is bulletproof, is destined to fly. That person sees every distrust they have of him, every doubt they show as a flag that increases his courage and makes his class emerge. Those of us who are purple feed on unbelief. We relish the doubts, the criticism, the scepticism, the envy of others. All of them are reasons to make progress. It doesn't kill us. It only gives us more wings to fly, more reasons to make our success resounding and enormous. If you, on the other hand, have the mindset of a white cow, you will continue to believe their criticisms and the distrust they have of you. Keep showing what you are made of. Show that you can, and if you prefer to do this and it helps you fly, visualize yourself being successful, materially and spiritually, while all of the people who had no confidence in you now share the crumbs that fall from your table.

One way to rebuild your context then is to convert the doubts, the bullying, the labels, the way they judge you into reasons to make progress. In general, all of these criticisms and doubts come from people who are authentic white cows, normal insipid beings who've never shown results and who are not worthy of being examples for you nor role models for growth. They are mentally aged with no greatness in their past and even less in their future.

The two examples above, show us, I repeat, that the past doesn't correspond to the future unless we continue to live in the past. Rebuilding the context implies a huge investment of energy and emotions.

I will say it a thousand times, when you change what you are, you change what you do. "Juan Diego, so is my secret to change what I am doing to see if I do better with something else?" No, the secret is in reinventing yourself and in not believing that today is equivalent to tomorrow. Going through a a transformation experience will make things different, striking, new, purple, magical, and you will be another person, perhaps a happier one. I can convert myself into whoever I want to be. Never forget that before being rich, you have to be.

And the second thing, don't scourge yourself. If success still eludes you, if you still haven't found your purpose in life or your "reason why," if there is still no abundance in your life, remember that the Universe won't hold back on anything. Do what you need to do so that good things come to you, and the main one is a determination that has been branded into you to say or to decree: "my happiness is not negotiable."

10

AND AFTER
THIS BOOK, WHAT?

In this final part of the book, I'd like you to begin to reflect on a question: when you die, how do you want to be remembered? What do you want your epitaph to say? I have thought about this many times throughout my life, and the answer revolves around changing through quantum leaps, finding a "reason why," having Level 10 motivations that nourish your desires and hunger to achieve your goals, and therefore, the determination to be wealthy and prosperous.

In my case, I know how I want to be remembered and what my epitaph will be like: "Here lies a man that made himself; a man who put himself to the test, a man who never wanted to die as coal because he always wanted to die as diamond."

From the moment I identified my purpose in life—to inspire and transform millions of people to be happier through better financial education and personal growth—I have obsessively dedicated every minute of every hour of every day to that, to *investing* in that goal. These pages have no other goal than that, and I am sure they have been revealing and inspiring and will reinforce your determination and make the inner purple you, your essence blossom. If you have not started down that road yet, I think that as of now you have the pro-wealth tools, strategies and habits to begin to make the changes needed in your life and thus achieve better income and quality of life. Don't let more time go by.

Starting now, there can be no more wasted minutes nor delays. Nor can you speak with limiting words that hold you back from building your own "reason why" any more. Don't let the negative thoughts and fears ruin the opportunity that life is giving you. Begin today to behave like the person you want to be, change what you have to change at the same time starting with the people you are around, the negative language you use, the states of low energy, making the same investments you always make and abandon your fears. Let this be the last gray picture of a white cow that the Universe takes, and let all the ones taken from now on shine with purple and happiness.

If you change who you are, what you do also changes. Do you want your business to grow? Start with your personal growth.

Nobody said that that it would always be easy to overcome your fears, tear down the social labels that weigh on you, stop using negative words and expressions of doubt, or to even see family and friends that prevent you from making progress less frequently. Rebuilding the context is essential. Encouraging pressing needs that force and induce you to find new sources of income is not easy either after we've spent years living the life of white cows and now aspire to the life of purple cows. My advice is simple: begin TODAY to be what you want to be because life is short and it would be very sad to die without having dared to be it.

Death, as we said in another chapter, is a powerful motivation. It makes us lay aside the "philosophy" of step by step and pushes us towards determination and change. Knowing that we have a limited amount of time in this life to do and be what we want to be leads us to make the quantum jumps. However, the majority of people are afraid of death for the simple reason that they have put off their dreams. When will you be purple, if you keep postponing them? That is why I always affirm that being poor when you have everything to be wealthy is an irresponsible thing to do to those you leave behind when you die. It is the kind of thing white cows do, not purple ones.

A better life is possible. Don't say what the majority does: "This is the life that I'm stuck with." I will help you to become purple.

Remember that ideas are the new name for money in the twenty-first century. So, if you have an idea in the making to start your own business, don't discard it because of fear or because toxic people tell you it is no good or, worse yet, that it's impossible. Don't let that be the reason. "Juan Diego, I have ideas but no one in my house believes me." Fine. Leverage yourself with that and afterwards, invite your detractors to a celebration with the earnings your business incurred and do this without rancor. It is important to have

Level 10 motivations in life. Because when you do, the defects, fears, and excuses are eclipsed.

The same thing happens with your own business. You make it successful when you have a strong need; when urgency knocks at your door, when the payment date for your mortgage or for tuition at your child's school approaches. But let's go beyond that. You, like me, are going to die, but don't let your work die. Make yourself immortal with something; leave a legacy of work. What is it going to be? Will it be your business, your books, videos, perhaps a foundation through which you will help others?

Many doubt you can do it. They despise and look down on you. I want you to silence them with your life. I want to see you in a supercharged mode.

It is possible that the greatest fear with respect to seeking a purple life is losing the "security" that a permanent job gives. The first thing to remember is that it is not permanent. Having what appears to be a permanent job or depending on a company or business that isn't your own turns out to be an illusion in the end. You die a little at a time over a lifetime when you work on something that you don't enjoy and for which you are poorly paid. Don't hasten your death nor feel remorse when that day comes because you haven't freed yourself from that mirage called "employment and fixed income."

I have always been interested in people building and finding sources of income apart from their wages. At one point in life, a job can help you get experience, save money, and perhaps accumulate capital. But a salary cannot always be the only source of income. Depending on that is to become used to a comfort zone where whether or not you do things well or whether or not you do what you love, you still receive money at the end of the month. A little, but it is money. Even worse, the days go by, the years go by and most people keep on waiting for a pension which, if it is paid, will be negligible compared to the time you dedicated to your job, time that is gone forever and that never allowed you to achieve your goals. Maybe you did fulfill other goals such as living to pay a mortgage. Very few become rich by depending on a salary.

So think about whether or not it is time to leave behind the boring and frustrating job you have or the one that, even though you like it a lot, doesn't give you the money you need to substantially improve your quality of life. Maybe it is time to throw the cow over the cliff, launch out into the streets of independence and the generation of your own resources. Forget the salary. The financial obsession of the purple cows and of the truly wealthy is passive income.

A salary and pension aren't enough to pay for the quality of life that someone who really aspires to be rich wants to have. If you have defined your purpose clearly, the "traditional savings culture" won't be enough to fulfill it. You will need to turn to a culture of investing in yourself, of generating more sources of income and, even better, of increasing your passive income over time. If a person has a habit of investing rather than of saving, he will have the capital that supports that desire to become more prosperous every day;

that determination to have a better quality of life, not "some day" but immediately after this is decreed.

Saving is putting the money in the bank, or under the mattress where it doesn't earn more money or earns only the minimum. We have already said it: in this era, money and technology should work for us, not the other way around. The days when people had to enslave themselves to a job they actually hated in order to save "little by little," look like a black and white film now. Today, money and technology are what should work to create true capital.

> **"Juan Diego, I'd like to be rich. Will I achieve that?" Start by replacing *I would like* with *I will*. That which you decree, you will accomplish more easily!**

When someone tells me that he came into the world to get money, I say: "You are wrong; money is only the consequence of what you do." Abundance of money is the logical consequence of something you do very well, and the fact that you work things out so that many people can get your product. Abundance of money is also the expected outcome of the opportunities that an informed mind takes advantage of. One of the fundamental changes you have to make in your life is to understand that you yourself are a product, in fact the most important one in your sales portfolio and one that is indispensable in the search for greater income. As such, when you overcome your fears, and I have already explained how to do that, you will discover that you have many talents and that you are probably good in things that others aren't good in. This is your opportunity to change from a white cow to a purple cow. Don't seek to have money. Seek to have ideas that produce it. Don't concentrate on the result, concentrate on the purpose.

This has a lot to do with thinking and developing ideas that will help thousands, millions, and have an impact on people's lives. The world outside is eager to buy and consume an endless number of things, and this is enhanced by Internet. This "outside" is no longer just our country but the entire region, all over the planet. This is our business reality, and it touches all of us without exception. So out "there" you have a captive market to satisfy with what you do very well. The number of people who see it will be directly proportional to the money you receive. And I am referring to taking advantage of social networks that we all use today.

The most deeply rooted popular belief that works against the desire to be wealthy is the one that says money is evil. How can anyone become a millionaire if, when I ask him what he thinks of money, he says: "It is a necessary evil?" Please, what necessary evil? Money is very important and if you have forgotten this, it is used to print Bibles and build churches. When someone says that money isn't a priority, I already know two things: This person is poor or will never be rich.

That is why I want the day to come when you buy what you want, what you like rather than what you can because "I can only afford this." I want you to stop asking: How much is it or why is it so expensive? Money isn't a barrier and if you want to be rich, you cannot continue to think of it as a scarce or limited resource but as something you generate yourself based on your aspirations and ambitions. Many were raised to believe that ambition is bad. But whoever said that led a very frugal life, not worthy of imitation. So don't be afraid of being subjected to pressure, nor of setting high goals. Let me warn you ahead of time: After this, you will NEVER be the same.

"My son, ambition is bad, we might lose you." "Dad, but I'm doing very well and I can help your church more." "In that case, go ahead, son."

Like a butterfly that was a caterpillar before, let yourself have the joy of changing, flying, and reaching your goals as I have done. Focus on your "reason why" and don't allow the fears to gain ground. Always use optimistic and winner's language. It's worth being recalled again and again: the achievement is not to get money in order to accumulate more and more all the time. Money is not the final goal. The profound and transcendent purpose of our lives is the goal to serve and to impact lives with money acting as the means whereby we achieve it in some cases, and in others, the happy outcome of developing that purpose. So yes, fly, but in search of your "reason why," to make an impact on people.

As we have already said: obtaining wealth, prosperity, and abundance is directly linked to the growth of each individual as a human being. That transcendent motivation should get us supercharged and make us shine in the distance, and then, when they ask us what is going on, we become so passionate that we overflow with the pleasure that it produces in us. The money will come to our door by itself when we really are investing in that great objective.

Remember: I want to see you supercharged. Supercharged! A purple cow doesn't ask destiny for permission. A purple cow is the destination.

Today is the first day of your new life, your new approach to money and ways get it. Look around and see how many people in the world cry and lament. You just get busy selling handkerchiefs.

In conclusion, I would like to thank you from the bottom of my heart for reading this book. All I have left to say is this: I shall see your motivations at Level 10. I shall see that your defects, your doubts, your fears are smaller than your ambition. I shall see that the stature of your critics—those who didn't have confidence in you, who told you that you were good for nothing—is lower than the stature of your dreams. And when we run into each other in any corner of the planet, i shall see you blaze in the distance and burning inside because you have such a huge torch and shed light on such a well-known destiny that it flows out of you. You could lie to me. We will see each other somewhere in this world, and you will avoid me if you fail to meet the challenge I have laid out in this book: may you find your "reason why," may you create your own business or if you already have one, make it grow and take off. The person you will never be able to lie to is someone who will accompany you to the tomb: yourself.

Remember: either raise the income from your business to the level of your dreams or you will have to lower your dreams to the level of your income. I want to see you in a supercharged mode. I want you to gobble up the world. I want you to leverage yourself off all of the doubters and go after what you deserve.

Who is afraid?

ABOUT THE AUTHOR

Juan Diego Gómez Gómez was a professor at the under-graduate and postgraduate levels for 12 years in the areas of Macroeconomy, Economic Policy, Investments and Financial Markets at the Universities of Antioquia, Pontificia Bolivariana, Eafit, the Engineering School of Antioquia, and Javeriana.

He is a business manager at Eafit University of Medellin and has a postgraduate degree in Finances from this same institution, studies in economy and economic development at the London School of Economics, at the University of London Birkbeck College, and Negotiation at Harvard University.

He was a broker in the Medellin Stock Market for five years, worked in the financial departments of Enka de Colombia, and Banco Industrial Colombiano (now Bancolombia) and was the director of planning for Corfinsura.

He was a columnist for *El Colombiano* and *La República* for a period of five years.

He is the author and co-author of several papers on financial topics for international events and has published five books: *Lectures on Economy and Finances* (1999), *Stocks, Theory and Practice in the Colombian Variable Income Market* (1999), *Investments and Capital Markets* (2000), *Financial and Economic Analysis* (2001) and *Investments over the Internet* (2004).

He has been a consultant on issues of voluntary pensions for Skandia and on investments and personal finances for Procter & Gamble as well as a speaker and academic coordinator for 75 seminars on investing over the Internet; 6 of them *online*, 64 seminars in person for groups of people and 5 for corporations (Uniban, ISA, Fondo de Garantías de Antioquia, Empresas Públicas de Medellín and Universidad Autónoma de Manizales).

In 2009, he inaugurated his seminar on Financial Freedom and Personal Finance. In 2011, the Training Program for Traders and the InvertirPorInternet.com site. In 2013, TuNegocioWeben1Day.com and the conference BE Extraordinary. In the 2014, there was GanarDineroConVideos.com and the Fewer Fears, More Wealth conference, and in 2016, the "How to Make Yourself Wealthy" conference.

He is currently the most influential youtuber in Latin America in terms of financial education and personal growth with more than a million followers on social networks and fifty million views on his YouTube channel InvertirMejorOnline.

www.InvertirMejor.com
www.InvertirPorInternet.com
youtube.com/InvertirMejorOnline
facebook.com/InvertirMejorOnline
Twitter: @InvertirMejor